# The Hampshire Moor

## BRIAN VESEY-FITZGERALD

*with twenty-seven illustrations*

## CASSELL

AND COMPANY LIMITED
LONDON · TORONTO · MELBOURNE
SYDNEY & WELLINGTON

*First published 1950*

SET IN 12 PT. GARAMOND
AND PRINTED IN GREAT BRITAIN BY
BUTLER & TANNER LTD., FROME AND LONDON
F.750

# THE HAMPSHIRE AVON

OTHER RIVERS IN THIS SERIES

*Already Published*

THE RIVER WINDRUSH

THE RIVER FOWEY

*In Preparation*

THE RIVER CONWAY

THE RIVER DOON

THE AVON AT CHARLTON

*To*

STEPHEN  GRAHAM

# CONTENTS

vii

# LIST OF ILLUSTRATIONS

ix

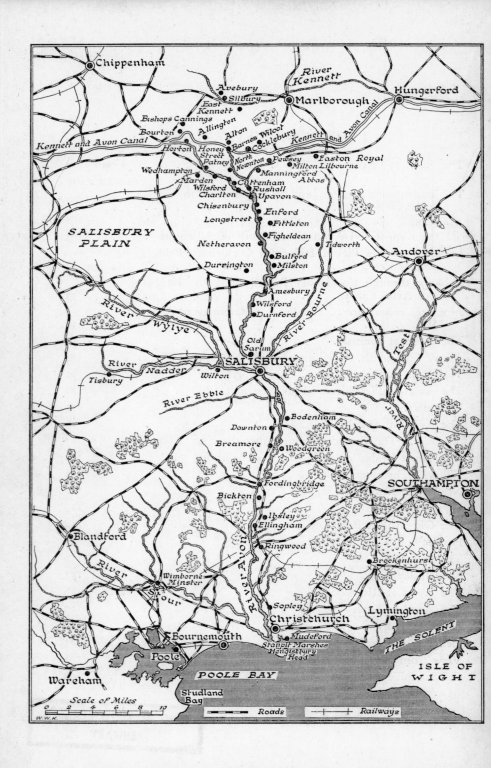

## CHAPTER I

## THE NORTHERN ARMS

You should, of course, start a river at its source. All the best people do. And has not Reginald Arkell pointed out that " to understand the course and current of a river, it is necessary to trace it back to its earliest beginnings—the spring in the hills, the little ditch trickling into the vale, the brook through the meadows, the tributary joining the parent stream, until, at last, we reach the river and the sea " ?

I knew all this, and I was determined to understand this river. But when I got out the Ordnance Survey maps, it did not seem at all clear just where the source was. So I wrote to the Ordnance Survey Office asking for precise details of the source of the river. They were very courteous about it all—and they were very frank. They did not know. They pointed out that there are two branches to the river, and, further, that these two branches branch, and in fact, they said, the actual source might be any one of a number of streams.

So I set out to explore for myself. And I have to admit that I have not found the source of the Avon. It might, indeed, be any one of a number of streams. Furthermore, I should not like to say that I found the actual source of all these streams. But I did have a very pleasant walk.

The Hampshire Avon divides just above the village of Upavon, in Wiltshire, at a place called Scales Bridge, which lies in the parish of Rushall. So I went to Pewsey by train and thence, having successfully thumbed a lift, to Upavon by lorry.

Upavon is a nice clean village with a very pleasant smell of cows, and it has an excellent inn. In this I enquired of the locals which branch of the river was the main one, an enquiry that produced a profound difference of opinion. No one had asked that question before and as so often happens when you ask a question about local topography there was a moment of stunned silence, while they tried to make up their minds whether I was pulling their legs or not, and then a whole wealth of information, most of it quite irrelevant, poured out and at times the discussion became distinctly heated. On the whole, opinion favoured the eastern branch, because on that arm stood Pewsey and Pewsey was beyond question the most important place on either branch. This branch was wider too, and flowed more swiftly (though while the breadth was generally admitted, the speed led to heated argument), and so it must be the main one. But when I asked where the river started, no one knew—and no one cared : sufficient that it did start—though one man did say that he thought that it joined the Kennet, and this set them all off on tracks I had no wish to follow.

Obviously, I thought, leaving the inn, the branch to follow first was the eastern one, and this had the added advantage that I would be walking through country that already I knew well. But when I came to Scales Bridge I was on the wrong side of the stream, and the light was failing, and so it was the western branch that I walked first.

The river here is undistinguished—no more really than a small brown stream—but beautiful with the Downs rising steeply on the one hand and the elm-studded Vale of Pewsey stretching away on the other. I slept that night in a hollow in the Downs above the village of Charlton. Not as good a place as I could have wished, but I had left it too late, and it was the best of a limited choice. For all that, I slept well and was warm, though the night was cold enough.

I woke at five, and lay for a moment or two listening to the birds. But you do not want to lie too long, nor spend too long packing up again. These early hours are the best in the day for moving : if you must cover ground (and I had to) then it is advisable to cover as much as possible before noon, even (if you can) before ten o'clock, and dawdle afterwards. Put your mind to it and your best foot forwards, and it is astonishing what ground you can cover between six and ten in the morning.

Below me, I could see the line of the river, beyond the cottages of Charlton. I crossed the road and went to it, and soon found a place suitable for a bathe. The water was surprisingly cold—it always is!—but there is nothing so invigorating as this early morning dip. I am not a believer in cold baths every morning in the home—I have known one or two he-men who have religiously taken them, and the only one who is still alive is an unhappy ill-tempered fellow—cold water is so much colder in a cramped bathroom. But on a walk I am a firm believer in bathing at least twice a day, if possible. It is good for the feet above all things. And, though the water is cold of an early morning, the activity of the body soon conquers chill. And then, the early morning by a stream is a good time to get your breakfast. Afterwards, if you have had your breakfast after that, or, if not, after the morning coffee, you can do your washing —the shirt, the socks—and dry them as the sun rises. Bathing at mid-day is tiring. That is the time for a sun bathe. But a bathe at night is magnificent, taking the tiredness from your legs and inviting the sleeping bag. But it has not the immense exhilaration of that first breath-taking jump in the early hours.

To save the towel—towels always take so long to dry—I dried by running up and down the field, and then, filling the drum with water from the stream, walked back to my camp. On the way, I passed a farmhand driving a lame cow, and he stared in blank astonishment as I said " Good morning ", too amazed even to acknowledge my greeting. When I looked back as I climbed to my hollow, he was still standing staring after me—and of his cow there was no sign.

The fire was easy to light and I had my coffee, and smoked a pipe, looking down on the village coming to life, and away beyond to trees and a small isolated hill, blue in the morning mist. Quiet and secure, it looked, sure of itself and its place and purpose, fitted to the contour of the land.

Quiet and secure. But it was not always so. Rather

3

more than a hundred years ago—in 1830 to be exact—
Charlton had its brief moment in the national eye. It was
grim in England in those days. The Napoleonic wars had
left us victors, but exhausted. We are so immersed in our
troubles to-day that we do not realize that it has all happened
before—that it happens after every great war—this paralysing
exhaustion of the victor. It is the final instalment of the
system of deferred payments by which triumph is secured.
There were, in the years following the defeat of France, the
twin crises of rising prices and vast unemployment—but
then the now familiar pattern of events lasted longer. From
the battle of Waterloo to 1830 wheat averaged sixty-seven
shillings, and that in a country where wages were very low
indeed. There was not much work to be had, and under
the old Poor Law the surplus population of parishes were
kept dragging stones on to the roads so that they might not
be kept in idleness. The rates were, as was inevitable,
crushing, and that affected the rent of the farms, which
meant that farmers could not employ as many men as they
would normally have done. And then, to make matters
worse for the farm labourer, the threshing-machine was
introduced. It takes a good deal to rouse the Wiltshire
farm labourer to violent action. But this did. Many saw
what little work they had disappearing. They formed bands
and roamed the countryside, destroying the machines and
leaving a trail of wreckage and fires behind them. Troops
were sent to quell the riots. Quite large numbers of troops
were gathered together in Wiltshire, at Devizes and Salisbury,
but the only engagement of this miniature civil war took place
at Charlton. A big band, several hundred strong, was surrounded. They were armed with pitchforks, but they seem
to have been overawed by the troops and did not use them.
There was no bloodshed except that one of their number had
an ear slashed off by a sabre stroke from an over-enthusiastic
young yeomanry officer. But the steps taken after the riots
had been broken (and they were broken here at Charlton)
were drastic in the extreme. Three hundred and thirty men
were arraigned at the next assizes : thirty-five were hanged

and eighty-three were deported for life, while most of the
rest were given terms of imprisonment.

I went down to the village and looked at the church.
I never miss going into the church of any village I pass
through :

> A church and a chapitle,
> Wonderly wel y-bild,
> With niches on everiche half,
> And bellyche y-corven ;
> With crotchetes on corneres,
> With knottes of gold,
> With gay glitering glas
> Glowyng as the sunne.

So, Piers Plowman. It is trite to say that the most precious
inheritances of the English are their poetry and their parish
churches ; trite but true. Religion may have lost its grip,
the churches may no longer be filled of a Sunday, but the
church is still the focal point of the village. The great
crises of human life—baptism, marriage and burial—are still
closely associated with the church, and, in the villages at
least, the church is still very closely connected with the daily
round of life. It may no longer be the centre of the social
life of the people—time was when it was school for the
children and club for the adults—it may have been superseded
in that respect by the inn, but still the average villager could
not imagine life without the church. Not that he ever consciously thinks about it, but it is there in the background of
his life always. Its bells measure out the days. More often
than not its clock is the only outside one in the village. It
is the rock of ages, the one really permanent thing in the
community. It is hallowed ground, not so much because
of its purpose as because of its associations. Generation
after generation have looked upon its fabric, and worked
upon its fabric, and left, bound up in its stones, something
of their personalities and more of their ideas both of this
life and of that to come.

If you want to learn something of the present life of a
village and its people, something of its inner personal history,

5

you will not of course go to the church. Nor will you go to
the parson or the squire. You will go to the inn. It is
in the inn that men talk, once the ice is broken, and the
true villager is always a fount of information about his own
place, and what they do not know at first hand they can
always supply from their memories of what their great-
grandfathers told their grandfathers, who in turn handed
the information on. It is thus that you will learn the names
of fields, and why this field has this name and that field that.
It is thus that you will learn why one arch of the old bridge
is a different shape and built of different stone from the
others. And in the village inn you may learn more of the
history of the squire's family than even the squire knows.
It takes time, but you do learn. From the church you get
a different knowledge : true historical knowledge, spiritual,
political and economic. It is all written in the stones as
plainly as in the pages of a history book. And if you are
fortunate enough to gain access to the parish records, then
what treasure is laid before you. Here is the very stuff of
life, the blood of history. Not nearly enough attention is
paid to our parish registers and parish accounts. It is true
that a certain number have been printed and so are preserved,
but the vast majority of the most valuable records of social
conditions are still uncopied, and likely to remain so. But
even if you cannot get a sight of parish records or accounts
(and probably you will not ; you probably will not have
time anyhow) there is history enough to be seen in the
stones by an observant man. For example, you may see in
many an old church the stones of the porch scored with
grooves. Those grooves were made by English archers,
the famous long-bowmen, for it was the custom to have
target practice on Sundays outside the church and the arrows
were sharpened on the entrance to the church.

It is intriguing to guess why a church was built just
where it stands and who first built it. In very few cases is
the original builder of a church known. The majority of
our village churches are of Saxon or very early Norman date
and presumably they owed their origin to some local lord,

THE JUNCTION OF THE EASTERN AND WESTERN ARMS OF THE AVON AT SCALES BRIDGE

ALONG THE WESTERN ARM, AT THE JUNCTION OF THE AVON WITH THE KENNET AND AVON CANAL, SOUTH OF ALLINGTON

serving as a chapel for himself and his dependents. But why were they built just there? What decided the choice of site? The village we see has grown up round the church. When first the church was built there would be open country where now are buildings: at any rate there would be no permanent buildings. But there must have been some over-ruling consideration that determined the builders to choose this or that site. In many cases there can be no doubt that the ground was already holy ground—it cannot be mere accident that so many of our early churches were built in the proximity of prehistoric mounds (in some cases, as in the Saxon church at Corhampton in Hampshire, actually on the mound itself)—the meeting place or the place of worship, or the burial place of an earlier religion. I find it exciting, standing before a village church, to realize that this ground has been put to much the same use for thousands of years.

The church at Charlton was once a chapel of Upavon. It is not by any stretch of the imagination a beautiful building, and it has been much restored, the work being done about the middle of the nineteenth century. "Restored": that is a word that has become a term of abuse, just as "Victorian" has. The expert on old churches, the lover of old churches, sees some restoration, sniffs in a superior manner, and passes on. Especially is this the case when the restoration is the work of the nineteenth century. It is a pity, I think. We need to readjust our ideas about restoration.

Very, very few of our churches have come down to us intact in their original forms. Many have known sudden change, but those that have not have been subject to a long process of structural evolution that has not finished even at the present day. And every one of them owes its preservation in some degree to the work and care of parishioners, who have protected them against the slow decay of time and the ravages of the weather, patching here and there. Let us remember, too, the part played by religious bigotry in the history of our churches. Religious bigotry is never a pleasant thing, but it becomes excessively ugly, and excessively cruel, when it is backed by greed. That has too

B

often been the case in this country. You can see the result
of pure greed in the monastic ruins left by Henry VIII.
Religious fanaticism burnt heretics alive (and did not forget
to confiscate their property !) and another sort of religious
fanaticism wrecked the interiors of sacred buildings (but did
not forget to sell the treasures. stolen !). The work of
Protestants in this way was sheer vandalism, and it was the
more ferocious because they half-believed in just those things
that they were destroying. The early Christians were no
better when they destroyed Pagan temples. The destruction
of St. Sophia, and some of the most wonderful sculpture
that the world has ever produced, during the fourth crusade
was quite as bad as anything that Cromwell and his roundheads
achieved. But Cromwell is nearer home and nearer our
own time. We can see the result of his religious zeal on
every hand. We can but guess at the beauty we have lost.

All our churches have been restored in some measure,
and we need to reconsider the prevalent fashion of abusing
restorers indiscriminately. Actually, of course, it is only the
restorers of the nineteenth century that come in for indiscriminate abuse. And that is because we are too close to
them to appreciate what they have done. You have only
to look at an old church to realize how completely insensitive
men of culture can be to the work of the men of culture
of the age before. Each generation takes a delight in dis-
carding the ideals of its parents. So we are indignant with
James Wyatt, and disparage his work. I must admit that
I dislike what he did at Salisbury and Durham and Lichfield :
I must admit that I dislike it intensely. But will the Englishmen of the twenty-first century dislike it ? Did the Hano-
verian admire the work of the Stuart restorer ? I think not.
So, while we revile anything that bears the mark of Sir Gilbert
Scott, let us remember that two hundred years from now
he may be much admired. The architects of the nineteenth
century could not have been wrong always.

Which one did the restoration in Charlton church I do
not know, and I did not trouble to find out. It is not the
work of a distinguished man, but it served a purpose—that

8

of keeping the church in being. It must have been in a bad way indeed to demand what was done. But there are fragments of the old church left and some of them are lovely— a carved string course under the east window, which is early fifteenth-century work, is worth more than the cursory appraisal I was able to give it. But I was supposed to be exploring a river, and it was high time I started.

I set off along the river bank. There were cattle in the fields, fine sleek-looking beasts that took no notice of me. I am always wary of cattle in fields, for their curiosity can sometimes be embarrassing, and then there is always the possibility of a bull. In fact I would much rather deal with a bull than a stallion—and I have had experience of both— but I would not seek a meeting with a bull if I could help it. And bulls on river banks can be a real menace. Arthur Ransome has written a most delightful essay on the dangers of fishing, and you will remember that that bull not only swam the river but surmounted no less than three stone walls in his anxiety to make a closer acquaintance with the fisherman. But a fisherman is lightly baggaged. A rod does not weigh much, the creel can be jettisoned—it is probably empty anyway. But a man with a rucksack is handicapped. A rucksack is not an easy thing to run fast in, and it is a very clumsy thing to have on your back if you want to get over a fence or a wall quickly. I was once crossing a field in Dorset when I aroused the curiosity of a shorthorn bull. I have been told that a bull in the company of cows is not dangerous, but I know now that that is an old wives' tale. This bull had plenty of cows to keep him company, but it was my company he sought. I got myself over a tall thorn fence only at the very last moment, and I have examined herds of cows in fields through which I want to pass with great care ever since. All along this stretch the cattle were fine pedigree animals, breeding in every line of them, as smooth and shining as though they had just been groomed. And this is as it should be, for this has always been a great cattle-breeding and milk-producing district. As early as 1850 a bull from Charlton was sold to America for £450, a high price for those days, and four years later from another farm in the neighbourhood seven cows and a bull were exported for £1,000.

But the river itself was dull. There was no movement of birds. In all the stretch from Charlton to Cuttenham Farm by Wilsford I saw only one moorhen and there appeared to be no activity of fish, indeed, one might have been forgiven for thinking there were no fish in the river at all. At Cuttenham the river divides, forming an island, and I followed the main stream, walking through a countryside that seemed quite deserted and silent. I have walked many streams in Britain and abroad, and never before have I come across a stretch so lifeless as this. There were no birds, no fish, no insects. It looked quite normal, but in fact it was abnormal. And it was all the more extraordinary because where the island ended, where the stream resumed one main course, there was a heron fishing, and from then on there were birds in plenty and insects on the wing, and sound from the banks and hedgerows.

At Marden the river divides, and I had to spend some time studying the map to see which arm I should follow. It was not at all easy to decide, for from here there are streams all over the place and many of them ultimately run on to join others, a veritable maze of waters, almost any one of which might be the parent stream. The arm running towards Beechingstoke, however, did not seem at sight quite so considerable a stream as that running towards Patney, and rightly or wrongly I took the Patney arm. In any case I wished to see the churches at Marden and Chirton, and they lay in that direction.

Marden church has a Norman chancel arch and a Norman south door, which was restored in the fifteenth century. Actually the whole church was rebuilt in the fifteenth century, and the chancel was again rebuilt in the nineteenth century. Of the fifteenth-century work the nave and the tower remain, though you would never guess that in fact the tower had been rebuilt in the nineteenth century. That this is so is due to the late C. E. Ponting, who did so much fine work for

Wiltshire churches. He took down the entire tower and rebuilt it ſtone for ſtone. Each ſtone was marked and a plan of the joints was made so that there should be no miſtake as to its position. Would that all reſtorers were as careful!

A mere half-mile or so further on is the church of St. John Baptiſt at Chirton, which is quite the moſt remarkable work in all northern Wiltshire, and in one way at leaſt unique in all England. There has naturally been a good deal of reſtoration, but none that is offensive. The church consiſts of nave and aisles with south door, chancel and weſtern tower. It is the nave that I imagine to be unique. It dates from the latter half of the twelfth century—probably not later than 1180—and it is complete with contemporary roof. There may be another such in the country, but if there is I do not know it. The south door is of the same date, but was reſtored in the fourteenth century. It is a pleasant and amusing doorway, carved with the heads of deer and birds and ſtrange animals that I was unable to identify with certainty, and also with human heads and hands. Whoever the workman was, he was certainly a ſtudent of human nature and he gave me a very amusing half-hour while I reſted my feet. But that is not all that is in Chirton church. There is a font. It is of about the same date as the nave—perhaps a little earlier—and is a quite magnificent piece of work. Circular in shape, it is surrounded by twelve arches, which hold the carved figures of the twelve apoſtles. They are all holding books including St. Peter, who rightly holds a key as well, and St. Bartholomew, who holds something that I could not recognize.

As I was reſting outside, and admiring the carving of the doorway, I was approached by an ancient. We held the usual English conversation about the English weather, the while he eyed my rucksack with unfeigned curiosity— hikers are not common in this part of the world I am sure, for that rucksack aroused curiosity all through this area— and then I led him on to the church. It was he who solved the myſtery of St. Bartholomew's burden. I asked him what it was.

" 'Is skin," he said, " they'm flayed the pore beggar, they did zo."

He seemed to be the sort of man who might have ideas about rivers too, so I asked him where the Avon rose.

" If 'ee means thic river," jerking his head in the direction of Patney, " tha's not the Avon. Thic river, zno, is Marden Bruk."

The Avon, it appeared, was the name of the river at Salisbury. The river from Upavon to the sea (not, I found out, that he had ever been to the sea in his life) was the Avon. But from here to the main stream was the Marden Brook, and the stream that flowed through Pewsey was the Deane Brook.

" 'Tidn' no manner o' use fer thee to talk, guv'nor. Thic Avon dussent rise nowhere in a manner o' speaking."

It was said with such decision and with all the authority of some seventy years lived in the district that I almost gave up there and then and went back to Upavon to start my walk downstream from there. It seemed the obvious solution : and it is the obvious solution to the Ordnance Survey's difficulty. But I was here now and I might as well go on. I asked him about the Marden Brook ; where did that rise ? That rose, it appeared, at Bourton beyond Bishop's Cannings. Now, Bishop's Cannings lies on the far side of the Kennet and Avon Canal, the canal which joins the Kennet (and thus the Thames) with the Bristol Avon, and this could only mean that the Marden Brook flowed from Bourton into the canal and then on to join the Deane Brook at Upavon. And, if this was so, then the Avon did join the Kennet, as the man in the inn at Upavon had said, though hardly, I thought, in the way he had meant. Anyway, it seemed worthwhile exploring further.

Patney is not a village to linger in. It has, I think, grown up round the railway station—Patney is a junction for Devizes—and it has all that atmosphere of impermanence characteristic of the immediate neighbourhood of railway stations everywhere. I should doubt if there are more than one hundred people living in Patney, and most of the houses look as though they experienced a regular and frequent change of tenants. I passed a cottage where a woman was trying to mow a lawn that had not experienced a mower for a long time, with one of those old two-wheel mowers. She had not got the box on, and she was shoving it forward to the full stretch of her arms and then pulling it back, remaining stationary herself and mowing in a series of jerks, going over the same ground again and again before she could get the tufts down. I looked at the lawn. It was not a big one. I leaned on the gate, and said it looked like hard work. She stopped and panted and said that it was. She spoke in the soft sing-song of the Cardiganshire hills, and I wondered what on earth she was doing here in the middle of Wiltshire in this dump of a village.

" Shall I do that for you ? " I asked.

" Oh." She was startled, " Oh, I couldn't bother you." She was suspicious, too.

" No bother," I said, unslinging my rucksack, " No bother at all. And you could feed me, you know."

That startled her even more. " Are you on the road ? " she asked, " You don't look like it. You're kidding me. Get along with you."

" Well, I am on the road in a manner of speaking "—a " manner of speaking " ; all these Wiltshire farm-labourers said it, and I was picking it up all too quickly—" I'm walking anyhow. And I'm hungry and I'm not kidding. I'll mow your lawn for you, and you can give me something to eat when I've done it."

She grinned. " Fair enough," she said, " Come in."

It was a small lawn, but it was a brute. I earned that meal. But it was a good meal, and hot strong tea afterwards. As I sat and sipped I asked her about the Marden Brook.

" It's no good asking me," she said, " I don't know round here at all. I've not been here long, and I've not got about much—just into Devizes sometimes for shopping and the cinema or the market. That's all. You'd better ask my husband. He's been here all his life and he'd know."

" How did you come to get here ? It's a long way from Cardiganshire."

" And how did you know I come from Cardiganshire ? " And then she laughed. " Oh, my voice, I suppose. Still, that might be anywhere in Wales, unless you know Wales very well. Oh, I was in the Waafs and stationed round here. And my husband works on the railway here. It's quite nice, you know, but, oh, so flat. I do miss looking up and seeing the hills."

The age-old plaint of those that once lived in mountains. And there cannot be any question about it. This Pewsey Vale is flat—not the dead flatness of Lincolnshire or the Fens, but flat indeed compared with the deep cleft hills round Pontrhydygroes with the great hump of Plynlymmon always in the background. But it was time to be moving on, and no time to be caught up in a conversation about the beauties of Cardiganshire and the hills.

" Rhaid i mi fynd yn awr. Mae'n dda gen i eich cwrdd. Prynhawn da."

Her eyes nearly popped out of her head. " Prynhawn da," she said, " Rwyn falch o'ch nabod."

I was out on the road and walking, when she ran to the gate, and a positive spate of Welsh came pouring out. But I went on. " Lwc Dda," she called, " Lwc Dda." (Good Luck. Good Luck.) And I turned and waved. She leant further over the gate and shouted :

" Arhowch funud. A gaf fi ddod gyda chwi ? " (Wait a minute. Shall I come with you ?)

I turned and waved again. And then there was a bend in the road, and open country before me.

On the map, streams are shown sprouting in all directions from Patney. There is one that rises near Wedhampton and another near Etchilhampton but the main one seemed to go on to a place marked Etchilhampton Water and it was near there that the brook from Beechingstoke, that I had left back in Marden, came in again, so I made for that. But I kept to the road, passing over the railway, for the road met the stream about a mile further on, and I could make haste over that mile. When I did join the stream again, it had shrunk to the dimensions of a ditch, but the water was flowing quite briskly, and I followed it north-westwards through pleasant fields until again it divided, and again I had recourse to the map. I was making for Horton—a distance of not more than two miles as the crow flies—for there I should pick up the two streams again, the one crossing the canal for Bishop's Cannings and the other a little to the east-wards crossing for Bourton.

Short of Horton there is yet another division—a branch going away westwards past Coate. This branch looked rather larger and stronger than that coming from Bishop's Cannings, and for all I know it may be the real source of the Marden Brook, but I negotiated the junction and kept to the Bishop's Cannings stream, not only because the old man in Marden had said so but also because it obviously sprang from the Downs rising before me, and that seemed a more likely source. It was not easy walking, and my boots were shockingly wet by the time I reached Horton. But it was dry and cosy under the bridge that carried the road over the canal, a good place for a camp.

Here you are right on the edge of the Vale of Pewsey. Bishop's Cannings lies, almost snugly, in a hollow below one of the highest and steepest escarpments of the Marlborough Downs. All through the Vale you have not been conscious of the Downs, but here they press in on you. And here you get Wiltshire scenery at its most characteristic—the long spacious sweep of bare windswept Down coming abruptly to the tall-timbered valleys. It is a quiet village, not beauti-ful but with that calm serenity that old ladies get that is so near beauty, and it has a really beautiful church. Once this was an episcopal village—the Bishops of Salisbury had a palace here—and before that perhaps it formed with the neighbouring village of All Cannings a royal estate. The church is one of the best in all the county of Wiltshire, a large cruciform early thirteenth-century building with a good tower and a stone spire of wonderful grace and height. The villagers are proud of their church and care for it, and there used to be a story in Devizes that they once manured the tower in the hope of stimulating the growth of a small pointed turret at the angle in emulation of the church at Devizes. Inside, too, the church is beautiful. There is some good Norman transitional work and good work also of the fourteenth and fifteenth centuries. Particularly do I like the low thick nave columns and the stone vaulting of the long chancel, and to crown it all there are lovely triple lancets in the chancel, in the west wall of the nave and in the transepts. I do not believe that they can be equalled in Wiltshire.

Aubrey tells us that in his day this village could have challenged all England at music, singing and football. There was one George Ferraby who was rector here in the reign of James I, and he was evidently a gentleman of character and initiative. For when the Queen was on the road from Bath he greeted her with his choir at the Wansdyke, which crosses the Downs just above the village, and they sang her a song of his own composition " to the great liking and content of the queen and her company ". Furthermore, he dressed himself up as a bard and his choir as shepherds. I do not know what the singing is like in Bishop's Cannings now. In most Wiltshire villages it is noteworthy for its heartiness rather than for its excellence.

I sat for some time in the churchyard—like most country churchyards in these days, rather unkempt, the grass too long and covering the graves—somewhat to the polite surprise of the rector, and then set off to find the source of the brook by Bourton, a hamlet a quarter of a mile or so further on, stopping for some minutes to admire the fine collection of staddle stones lining the drive to the front door of Mr. Coombe's farm. Just beyond Bourton, where the road runs on to Easton Farm, the brook starts : so small and insignificant that you might easily mistake it for a ditch. This presumably is the source of the Marden Brook, though I must say that the brook at Bishop's Cannings itself looks more likely. Having found it, and more than a little disappointed, I returned to the village, and took the road back to Horton.

It was market day in Devizes, and no amount of banging on the door of the inn at Bishop's Cannings would bring response, and I was thirsty, which was why I went back to Horton to the Bridge Inn. That was open, being on the road from the villages of the Vale to Devizes, and though the landlord was absent, there was a woman to serve me and to talk while I drank. All morning I had been conscious of distant thumps, felt on the eardrums rather than heard, and periodically as I was walking there would be a rattling overhead and then silence. That rattling was horribly reminiscent of shells going over, and, sure enough, she told me that they were firing on the plain, but she could not tell me what the rattling was nor where they fell. But she could tell me where a lot of bombs—our own bombs dropped in practice—fell and she was only too willing to recount tales of damage. Of damage I saw no signs whatever, but that thumping lasted throughout the day—a present and sinister reminder that peace is but a frail plant.

I was now back on the canal. The obvious thing to do was to retrace my steps to Upavon and then to follow the course of the Deane Brook. But the canal was inviting and even more inviting was the bare road under the Downs, and by walking eastwards through the Vale by road and canal I would meet the Deane Brook again at Pewsey. It would be better than retracing my steps, even though it was not strictly following the Avon, but I have never been one to keep strictly to the rules.

The road edges the foot of the Downs through wide open unfenced country. It is not a road that anyone wanting to get to the other end of the Vale quickly would use, and that makes it all the better, for it fits both the mood and the pace of the walker. Moreover, it is lifted a little above the Vale, so that you get a fine prospect over it, while you have the steeps of the Downs, earthwork fringed, for company on the other hand. It is a hedgeless road all the way—for much of it there is not even the barbed wire so beloved of the farmer—and the grasses ramp and there are dandelions in multitudes. Rooks rise and caw and follow you for a

space and settle and caw : great flocks of rooks, and a few
crows and rather more than a few jackdaws. But on the
whole of this stretch I did not see a magpie, where in the
more sheltered country of Hampshire I would have seen
many. I have always maintained that the magpie is a bird
of the tall hedgerows and the grasslands. It has increased
enormously in recent years—just before the war it was comparatively a rare bird, so that you were always looking for
the second one that would bring you luck and as often as
not being disappointed—and that is, perhaps, due a little to
the shortage of gamekeepers. But more it is due, I am sure,
to the cutting down of the hedges and the ploughing up of
the grass. The birds have been driven into more confined
spaces, and there undisturbed they have bred prolifically,
but I doubt if the increase is really so great as is commonly
maintained. I believe rather that the bird is easier to see
and that it is now seen by many who never saw it when
England was rich in hedges. I have been gently taken to
task for this view in a Fourth Leader in *The Times*, but even
that has left me unrepentant. Here, at any rate, was a
magpie-less country.

There were buntings perched on the telegraph wires at
regular intervals, but the birds that shared this wide open
country with the rooks were the skylarks. Skylarks everywhere and all the time. I know no music of the day that I
would rather hear than the hymn of the skylark, no music
of the night that I would rather hear than the praise of the
woodlark. I know that the nightingale is a master (though
I think myself that a good blackbird in the full passion of
love is the master of any nightingale), I know that there are
many song birds that are more highly rated by the experts
than the humble skylark, but I wonder if this is not just a
little because the skylark is so common and also just a little
because to hear the skylark at his best you must spend days
on the bare and windswept tops, just as to hear the woodlark
at his best you must spend nights in the open and awake ?
At any rate I love the skylark. He is company in empty
places and in all weathers. There is no day throughout the

year when you may not hear him sing, and few hours in the day—if there are any. His is a song that lifts the heart and the feet.

It is only in solitary and treeless spaces that you can get to know the skylark and his ways. There are plenty of sky-larks in the valleys but in the valleys the skylark is no more than a flickering black speck against the sky, and when he drops he drops like a stone to the earth and is lost in the long grass. But on the Downs you can watch his whole life, on the ground and in the sky, and on the Downs you will soon come to the conclusion that there is no bird in all Britain that has the skill and power of the skylark on the wing—and when I say that I remember the mastery of the buzzard and the knot and the golden plover, and all the birds of prey and all the waders of the seashore. Remember-ing them all, I say that there is none that exceeds the skylark in mastery of the air.

Watching the skylarks and listening to their song, picking up one as I left one behind, the miles rolled by unnoticed. Well as I knew this road—and that is well indeed, for there was a time when I must have passed along it twice in the day at least once a week—I was past the turning down to Allington, past the long buildings of All Cannings Cross Farm, past the turning to Stanton St. Bernard (at whose Rectory I used once to go to Shakespeare readings : that was in the days before the regular bus services, and that was one of the ways one amused oneself in the country in the winter, and it was not all that long ago), I was at the turning to Alton Barnes before I could shake myself free of the magic of the skylarks.

There are two Altons—Alton Barnes, which lies a little off he road and down towards the canal, and Alton Priors, which lies on the road and about a quarter of a mile further on—and they are very old. They are mentioned in a Saxon land charter of 825, and again in Domesday Book. There is a little church at Alton Barnes that is well worth a visit, and is very little visited. It is tiny, just a nave and a chancel (no porch) and the nave is only twenty-five feet long and

19

about half that in width. But it is very very old. There has been a lot of restoration work done at one time and another, but the walls are all Saxon work with the long and short quoins all the way up. There is nothing else in Alton Barnes—the name, by the way, has nothing to do with St. Bernard—to delay the visitor. Before the last war it was just a quiet little hamlet—neither beautiful nor ugly—but now opposite it are the remains of an aerodrome. The relics of war are never pleasant to look upon, but there are few things more depressing than a disused aerodrome with its shells of hangars, its rusted wire, its broken concrete roads with the weeds bursting through. The notices so lavishly displayed by the Air Ministry—Air Ministry Property—Keep Out—are quite unnecessary. No one in his senses would want to go in. But the shambling wreckage reflects no credit on the department that owns the ground, and the waste of ground that might be producing food and employing people reflects no credit on a Government that is continually calling for more and greater production.

Alton Priors church is scarcely worth a visit, though it is now the church for the combined living of the two Altons. It was in the red brick rectory of Alton Barnes that Augustus Hare lived. No doubt some of his " sermons " were delivered in Alton Priors, but I imagine that most of them were given to the little congregation at Alton Barnes. The " Alton Sermons " were once very popular, and still bear reading. Hare, who died very young and who is buried with Keats at the foot of the Cestius in Rome, was obviously an unassuming person, content with an isolated living in what was then a very backward part of the world, but if you read his *Sermons to a Country Congregation* you cannot escape the conclusion that here was a man in the great tradition of English letters.

Towering above the Altons is a White Horse, which must command one of the most extensive views of any White Horse, for it can be seen quite distinctly from Old Sarum twenty miles away across the Plain. It is not an old White Horse—very few of them are, and you can often tell them by their tails, for docking of horses is a comparatively recent,

and brutal, fashion—but was begun in 1812 at the command
of one Robert Pile, then the tenant of the Manor Farm at
Alton Barnes. Pile, with a lack of care quite foreign to the
normal run of Wiltshire farmers (than which there is no more
canny race) contracted with a journeyman painter to do the
work and paid him twenty pounds in advance. The painter
pegged out the horse—fifty yards from head to tail—set
some men to work, and decamped with the cash. Pile,
however, went on with the work and it was eventually
finished, though at considerably greater cost than that first
estimated. And now, travellers on the British Railways
(Western Region) point it out to each other as the site of
one of Alfred's famous victories over the Danes. There is,
however, a further landmark on these Downs that is really
old. As you climb up from the White Horse to Milk Hill
(and here you are nearly one thousand feet above sea level)
you come to the oldest dew-pond in Britain of which there
is any known record. It used to be called the Oxenmere
and it is mentioned in the Saxon land charter of 825. As
with White Horses, comparatively few dew-ponds are really
old, but here is one that does suggest that the art may go
back a long time, though not perhaps to early Bronze Age
times as is so often suggested. Dew-ponds do not always
hold water, of course, though they are popularly supposed
to do so, and on this visit of mine there was nothing to
show that so famous a dew-pond was here beyond a shallow
depression and a rather soggy bottom. Perhaps this, like
so many others, is now derelict. Time was when dew-ponds
were one of the features of our chalk hills, but they do
require some care, and in these mechanized days care is a
scarce commodity.

At the eastern edge of Alton Priors the Ridgeway comes
off the Downs to meet the road. Once, presumably, there
was a track across the Vale and then it climbed again over
Wilsford Down and up on to the Plain, but now no track
is visible anywhere in the Vale. But from the road at Alton
Priors it is plain enough climbing up the hill to join the
road below Adam's Grave, and it is plain again where it leaves

this road by the ancient earthwork. And temptation struck me again. It was no business of mine to walk this—it had no connection with the Avon, save that the Avon must take some waters from these chalk hills (or so the tempter whispered), and I was supposed to be exploring the Avon and not prehistoric tracks on the Downs. But from the top here you do get a marvellous view over all the Vale of Pewsey and across Salisbury Plain (on a clear day you can see the spire of the cathedral, a needle at the far end of it) and, at least, from the top I could see the country I was to walk, or some of it. And anyway, this was country I knew and loved and wanted to see again. To Adam's Grave I went. And as I walked I put up hares. The Down was alive with them. I do not know how many for I did not count, and should have lost count if I had, but hares everywhere, starting up and zigzagging away in front of me up the hill. I reached Adam's Grave and looked back.

The ground fell steeply away below me. If you come from Salisbury on the ancient track, just the same thing happens, the ground falls steeply away. The valley that lies below these two steep escarpments is the Vale of Pewsey, the Golden Vale. The Vale of Pewsey divides upper from lower Wiltshire, making two broad Downland countries of what should be one. From nowhere can you see it better than from Adam's Grave, surely the most grandly sited long barrow in all England.

You are sitting here on the edge of the Marlborough Downs, and it is—this stretch between Tan Hill and Martinsell—about the only real edge these Downs have. There is a northern scarp between Fiddler's Hill and Liddington, but it is nothing like so fine as this; steep, even rugged, yet beautifully moulded and softened, a great series of indented bays and jutting headlands standing out over the Vale. Perhaps you get a better view of the Vale from Knap Hill, on the other side of the road just opposite Adam's Grave, from one of the ramparts of the Neolithic Camp. I have heard people say that from there you get a better view of the chequered fields of the Vale, a better appreciation of their

LOOKING TOWARDS PICKED HILL FROM COCKLEBURY BRIDGE, NEAR WILCOT

LOOKING
THROUGH
COCKLEBURY
BRIDGE ALONG
THE KENNET
AND AVON
CANAL

enormous size. Maybe : I have tried them both often enough, and I prefer Adam's Grave, for there you feel perched on an eminence, suspended above the earth, and from there you can look along to the long green line of Rybury Camp, and feel yourself part of ancient things.

And the Vale ? Cobbett wrote of it : " This is certainly the most delightful farming in the world. No ditches, no water-furrows, no drains, hardly any hedges, no dirt or mire even in the wettest season of the year." Well, I have lived in the Vale and I would not care to go as far as that. But it is the richest land in England. The Vale is nowhere more than five or six miles wide between the Marlborough Downs and Salisbury Plain, but those few miles are the richest in grassland and in corn and in stately elms of any land in England. That at least Cobbett knew.

And the Vale is wide enough for a man not to feel shut in. I was born in a mountainous country, and I have never felt shut in, even in the narrow rock-bound valleys of true mountain country with the great hills rising abruptly on every side. But men who have not known mountains from infancy do feel shut in even in the small valleys of the south of England. I have heard a man complain of that in a valley of the Sussex Downs. Here no man could : he might feel enclosed but not shut in. He would always be conscious of the Downs on either hand, but he would also always be conscious of their tops. He must always see the distant Downs whenever he raises his eyes. " I will lift up my eyes unto the hills." No man, living in this Vale, could fail to gain from the nearness of those rounded hills. Just to see them is to drink in something of their slow serenity.

On this day, the sun was frequently obscured by clouds. There was a fairly strong westerly breeze driving clouds over the valley so that there was sunshine and shadow always climbing the downs and racing over the fields. The colours were constantly changing. The elms dark and the ash and willow light against them, and then all dark and tarnished. And from above the Vale looks heavily wooded, so that it is quite difficult to pick out the villages. It is lovely so.

But the real time to see the Vale from Adam's Grave is at summer's passing. Then you may watch the changes of colour on the cornfields as the harvesting progresses, the change of colour as the wind stirs the ears, the different colours of crops at different stages. No man knows the full beauty of England until he has sat on Adam's Grave at summer's passing.

Look behind you, and the horizon is filled with the line of the Wansdyke. The Wansdyke is a deep ancient trench between great embankments. It runs parallel with the Vale, but you cannot see it from the Vale floor, because some of the tops of the headlands that push out into the Vale are higher than this great earthwork. All the same, whoever planned it kept it as high as possible, digging where the deep hollows between the jutting headlands would not make it bend to avoid them. It emphasizes the immensity of Downland, rising and falling with the Downland curves, keeping always to its own course and yet always in harmony with the natural curves of the hills. So much in harmony with the Downs is it, that it seems that they have taken it to their heart. At least they are one now in spirit, for the growth of centuries has removed any irregularity it once had, though for centuries yet it will be recognizable as the work of man, and now the grassy, sheep-cropped banks, wind-blown, sun-baked, rain-swept, are part of the downland turf. For sixty miles it runs across the face of Downland—though you cannot now follow it all the way (I have tried)—and for what purpose it was built we do not know. At the very earliest it is late Roman, but most authorities agree that it is post-Roman. It faces northward—many people think that it was built to ward off attack from the south—and at first sight it seems evident that it was designed as a line of defence, perhaps against the Saxon invaders. But it runs pretty well from Inkpen on the Hampshire-Berkshire-Wiltshire border to Bath, and that, it seems to me, is a very long line to build against Saxon invaders : one, moreover, quite impossible to man efficiently. It is true that parties of Saxons did come up the Thames, but they were not sufficiently well established to attack all along a line that length, and, furthermore, there would in those days have been only certain places—and those comparatively few—at which attack would have been possible, for much of the country below the ridge was then impassable. Moreover, such a defence line leaves out of account altogether attack from the south. Approach from that direction would then have been at least as easy as from the north, and we know that there were Saxon raiders along the south coast who used the rivers to make entry to the interior. I am no archæologist, but I must say that the suggestion of a defence line against Saxon raiders from the north does not appeal to me at all. For I do not myself believe that there was ever a bloody Saxon invasion. I do not think they overran the country by force of arms, but that it was a more or less peaceful penetration. I think it more probable that it was built as a frontier. We know little of what happened in the years immediately following the Roman withdrawal, but it is quite certain that the Dark Age in Britain was not so dark that there was no social or tribal organization. Romano-Britons and Roman-trained Britons must have been left in plenty, and the country must soon have been parcelled out between various strong men, small princes ruling small countries. The line of the Wansdyke, it seems to me, is more the line of a frontier than the line of a fortification.

Running through the Wansdyke, a matter of a mile or so from Adam's Grave, though you get on to that ancient track but a quarter of a mile up the road, is the Ridgeway. And again temptation prodded me. It's only a little way further, said the tempter. And now you are up here, you might as well go on : it's really all a part of the Salisbury Plain civilization anyway. And so on. But, if truth be told, I needed no tempting. Once on the Ridgeway I had to go on, for the track has that sort of fascination, and I am in any case quite unable to withstand the lure of a road winding over the hills.

This track has become known as the Ridgeway, but in fact it is of course only one of many ridgeways running over the uplands of Britain. Years ago I bought *The Green Roads of England* by Hippisley Cox, and with its aid I have explored quite a few of them. But it is only on the tops of the Downs that they may be followed easily, for there they have not been distorted or obliterated by agriculture. In the valleys, as with both arms of the Ridgeway, they have often disappeared altogether. The great through ways of the chalk country, and especially those linking Wessex with Norfolk and the coast of Kent, are the easiest to follow and the easiest of all is this ancient green track, the Ridgeway. For much of its length north of Avebury it is two roughly parallel tracks, the one keeping to the crests of the Downs being the Ridgeway, the other following the lower slopes being known as the Icknield Way. It has been suggested that the higher track was for use in the winter months, the lower one for use in the summer months when the spring heads would have dried up, and that seems a reasonable enough suggestion. The crest track is very very old indeed : it was certainly in use during the last centuries of prehistoric Britain, and there are indications that it is much older even than that. While you can follow it fairly clearly as far as the Thames, beyond that only the Icknield Way can be followed with any certainty to the Norfolk coast near Hunstanton. South of Avebury, however, it is only the crest track that can be followed and that is lost in the Vale of Pewsey. However, there are tracks rising out of the Vale on the southern side, and one of these, running past Ell Barrow, takes you on to Old Sarum and the junction of many tracks. There is another gap here—if you wish to continue southwards—but then you can pick up tracks again, and with a good deal of guesswork here and there, follow them down to the coast above Seaton. I have at one time and another walked most of this area on tracks. But I am not suggesting that there is one track from the Norfolk coast to the south coast above Seaton, that there was ever one Ridgeway joining the two. There was never, I am sure, a single ridgeway between the two—probably the longest single route was the Harrowway or Hard Way, and much of

26

that can still be followed—but rather many hill-top tracks that led the one into the other. Certainly the Ridgeway can only be said to run from the northern escarpment of the Vale of Pewsey to the Thames fords by Streatley, and all the popular prolongations of the route, both north and south, should be looked on with suspicion.

But here, above Adam's Grave, the track is clear enough as it runs down to East Kennet, and very good walking it makes too, soft to the feet and the air exhilarating. It is a lonely unpopulated country. Richard Jeffries wrote : " Mile after mile and still no sign of human life—everywhere silence, solitude. Hill after hill, and plain after plain." And it is just the same now. The only human being you are likely to see is a shepherd. The only sounds you are likely to hear (save the aeroplane, which is now ubiquitous) are the bleating of sheep, and the song of the lark, and the mew of the kestrel, and the soft sighing of the wind in the grasses. There were wheatears and whinchats too, more conspicuous in one way than the larks, for they draw the eye as they flick to the top of a rabbit burrow or a tussock of grass. You cannot help seeing them whereas you have got to scan the sky for the singing lark. There were starlings also, and this is not always so. There were starlings because there were sheep. Whenever the sheep are on the Downs, the starlings are there in their company. But if the sheep are not up on the tops, you can walk all day and not see a starling.

There are not so many sheep as there used to be. And that is true of all the southern Downland country. I can remember when I was a boy the great flocks of sheep on the Downs above Winchester, and all along the Sussex Downs, and even greater flocks on Salisbury Plain. These are some of the finest sheep walks in the world, and when the sheep walked them the turf was lovely, soft in texture and of the most delicate shade of green. I can remember Salisbury Plain when it was green. But now it is but a poor coarse yellowish-green : the army and the cow have replaced the sheep to all intents and purposes and the countryside has suffered. Much of England's prosperity and greatness was built up on sheep. It was sheep that built the great churches of East Anglia and the Cotswolds, just as it was sheep that made the fine pastures that ensured the prosperity of the villages. Arthur Young wrote of these Downs : " I never saw so good sheep-walks as all this country ; the verdure good, and the grass, in general, fine pasture." Neolithic man seems to have farmed swine on these Downlands, but from the Middle Bronze Age without a break until quite recently it has been sheep, sheep, sheep. And with the passing of the sheep has come agricultural depression. You can get milk off the Downs, it is true, but with it you get coarse grasses and weeds, and all the milk in the world will not bring British agriculture back to the level of prosperity it enjoyed in the days of the sheep. For you get more from the sheep than mutton and wool—economic conditions weigh now against us in both those respects—you get also the Golden Hoof, and that is the most important of all the benefits the sheep confers on its owners.

But there are still sheep on the Downs. I saw some on this day, and I like seeing sheep on the Downs, not only because they ought to be there, but also because they show Downland in its true scale, which is a thing that, without them, is hard to appreciate. The flock is spread loosely over the down. They cover a large area, and that and the great width of the Downs and the great expanse of sky above them makes you lose all sense of proportion, so that you do not realize how great an expanse it is, for you have lost account of distance. It was so with me on this day. There was a flock of sheep grazing. I looked and thought that it was not a large flock, but that it was a small flock well spread out. I did not count them, but that was the impression I received. And then the shepherd and his dog appeared over the brow. When he got fairly close to the nearest sheep he sent his dog to work. In a few moments that flock was gathered together and then I saw that there were several hundred of them, a grey mass standing huddled together without apparently an inch of room between any two of them. And suddenly the down that had seemed small and filled with the few sheep scattered here and there about its face was vast and empty. The flock began to move, the shepherd in front and the dog behind circling from one flank to the other. I do like to see a shepherd leading his flock. It is becoming less and less common, though once it was the normal practice, and I wonder if this is because there are fewer and fewer real shepherds in the country nowadays. Shepherding used to be an inherited profession, son following father, and that it most certainly is no longer. There are few more fascinating sights than a flock of sheep on the move. They walk, it is true, but the movement is like that of water. A flock of sheep flows slowly. And, as with water, the shape is constantly changing, now wide, now narrow, now no more than a tight circle. But whatever the shape, it is rare indeed, looking at a flock moving over the Downs away from you, to see green among the grey. Always the sheep are tightly packed. And watching, I realize again how immense these Downs are. They rise to the first crest, the shepherd now dwarf-size, rise and disappear, and I had not realized how far away that crest was. I had not, indeed, realized that there was a crest there at all. And shortly they appear again, now no more than a flat grey smudge, the shepherd a black dot, breasting the rise to the horizon. And then they are gone, and I am left alone, and suddenly I feel very small indeed.

With the sheep went the starlings. But there were still the larks and the rooks. The full ecstasy had gone from the larks, but yet the air was full of song, for it was a bright sunny day, and despite the wind (there is always a wind up here) it was really hot. Had the sun been hidden the larks would have done no more than rise twenty yards or so, singing as they did so, and then dropped silently, but always there would be larks for company rising before you as you walked. But on a sunny day they rise to almost as great a height as in spring, and they sing as they fall again to earth. It was a hot enough day to make me want to sit down and cool off after the climb. I chose a place where I looked down on a wide hollow with a large patch of ragwort.

Ragwort is a pernicious weed, but its bright yellow is one of the very few notes of pure colour on these Downs, and I am grateful for it. Here and there on the slopes the green turf was scarred white to the chalk. Man-made scars these, and you will always find them on the highest and steepest slopes, where the turf is short and olive-green in colour from the grazing of the sheep. There are not very many of them, and the largest is no more than a few square yards, which means that they look like little white dots on the hillside, but it does not matter how small they are, the sun will seek them out and make them gleam and sparkle so that they catch the eye from a mile or two distant. Olive-green, the turf, but how many shades of olive! Grey it would look in the sunlight, and then there would be a cloud and the grey would go and the green would be dark. But always it was darker where the crest of the down carved the sky, lighter where the slope dipped to a hollow. The short, close-cropped, olive-green turf ended where the slope dipped to the hollow. In the hollow the grasses had grown tall and were dressed with long ripe plumes : plumes of many different colours, from the palest oatmeal through honey to a brown that was so warm that it was almost auburn. And the breeze gave voice to the plumes, a dry soft rustle that was more nearly the voice of the wind than theirs. And as they swayed and bent over new colours would appear, so that I looked across a moving sea of warm browns to the cold olive-green above.

But there are, of course, other flowers on Downland besides the ragwort and the grass plumes. Downland, indeed, has a multitude of flowers : the mauve of scabious, the purple of knapweed, the richer purple of thyme, the purple-blue of the bell-flower, the pink of centaury, the blue-purple of gentian, the blue of rampion, the true pure blue of harebell, the yellow of rock rose, the white of eye-bright. Flowers in multitude, yes, and their numbers must modify, and even change altogether the tones of Downland turf. And yet you have to look for them. They are not bold ; they do not stand up and boast as does the ragwort. You must look for them, and yet, close to, they are prominent enough. All, that is, save the yellow rock rose, which is overhung by the grasses, and the white eyebright, which is a very tiny flower, shrinking close to the ground. But the others are large enough to be noticed, and they are not because their blues and purples blend with the general tone of the countryside.

There were many butterflies about. Small heaths, blues, skippers, and they were in numbers. But they are all small butterflies and, except for the blues perhaps, easy to overlook. Indeed, not long after this day I heard a man bemoaning the shortage of butterflies this year, when I had been looking at large numbers of them, but he was meaning only the large and brilliantly coloured species, like the red admiral and the peacock and the painted lady, and he was thinking only of butterflies in gardens. These small butterflies may not be so interesting in colours, but they are certainly no less interesting in habits.

Watching the small heath, I found that it was a more constant percher on the grass heads than the blues and the skippers. There were no small coppers here as there would have been on the Hampshire Downs a little further south, but there were still a few dingy skippers about, and this was surprising, for it had not been a hot enough summer to encourage a second brood (as sometimes happens) and as a rule you do not find dingy skippers on the wing after the first week of July. Yet these were obviously first brood members—you could tell that by the faded tattered wings—and I can only suppose that there had been some delay in emergence owing to the bad weather earlier in the year. I watched one perch for a moment or two on a grass plume, and it kept opening and shutting its chequered wings just as it would have done in early summer, a movement that always seems to me to be displaying. The small heath is quite different in habit. Perched, it will usually fold its wings vertically over its body so that only the undersides can be seen. This is popularly supposed to be a protective movement, so that the undersides, by harmonizing with the surroundings, may conceal the creature from the eyes of an enemy. But when you come to look at them you also come to doubt that. There is no doubt about it, the small heath at rest in the daytime is quite noticeable. The brown of a part of the upper sides of the upper wings shows plainly through, and, if the sun is on it, it is almost orange. Moreover, the black eye-spot near the tip of the upper wing is also quite noticeable. And, if it is noticeable to me, a mere human with the limited eyesight of a man, how much more noticeable it must be to the keen eye of a bird. (It is said that when the butterfly goes to bed—that is about five to half-past five o'clock by the sun in August—it is not noticeable because the upper wings are thrust so far back that only the tips show above the inconspicuous lower wings, and then the brown part is invisible. If that is so, and I am sure that it must be, though I have not always observed it myself, then it would appear that the full armour of protection is needed when asleep, is needed after sundown. But I confess that I am at a loss to name the enemy against whom this armour of invisibility is required, though I could easily name a number of enemies abroad in daylight against whom no such measures are taken.) And it is just the same with the blues. There were three blues here, flying in the sun— the common blue, the chalk-hill blue and the Adonis blue. I know quite well that it is often very difficult to tell the difference between the chalk-hill and the Adonis on the wing, but I had a good view of these and there was no doubt whatever. The chalk-hill male is the blue of the sea and the female is satin brown ; the Adonis, free from variation, is a lovely sheeny blue, lilac rather than sea, and the female has a quite distinct blue dusting on her satin brown. The common blue is, of course, blue beyond a doubt—the blue of sunlight compared with the twilight of the holly blue.

Watching the blues—mainly common blues—I wonder again about colour and protection. For the most part these blues would settle on the grass heads, though a few would settle on the hard brown heads of plantains. There was plenty of the smaller field scabious about and had they

settled on the flowers they would have matched their surroundings much better than they did the grass heads and the
brown bents.  There is much silvery-blue on the undersides
of the wings that would have matched the colour of the
blossom fairly well, for the lesser scabious matures its seeds
in a burr, which passes through a series of colour from
green through lavender to grey and brown.  But I saw no
butterfly on the scabious burr—perhaps it is too prickly?
—nor yet one on the blossom.  But the larger scabious
blossoms and the knapweed are used freely.  The more I
think about it—and the oftener I watch—the less do I believe
that the butterfly relies on the mask of colour for protection.
I am sure that it does not do so during the daytime, and at
night it would surely have no value.  It is the mice and the
reptiles and such like that are seeking prey after the sun has
gone down, and for protection against them the butterfly
relies not on colour-masking but on height.

There is, of course, the fact that when asleep the butterfly
—not always, I think, but more often than not, the usual
but not invariable practice—lowers the folded upper wings
and thrusts them back until only the tips are showing.  But
I think that the object of this movement is not to harmonize
with the environment but to economize the amount of wing-
surface exposed to the weather.  I have watched both small
heath and common blue in the rain.  They do not adopt
the same position.  The small heath sleeps horizontally, like
a man ; the common blue sleeps vertically.  But each lays
back the upper wings until only the tips are showing above
the lower ones.  They are no more difficult to see like this—
with a little practice anyone with normal eyesight can dis-
tinguish a small heath at three or four yards distance, even
during a rainstorm.  But when you examine one closely you
begin to realize the reason for those folded-back upper
wings.  They are so tightly folded that they form a sharp
edge like a steeply falling roof.  The rain rolls off.  So, you
may examine a small heath or a common blue in a drenching
rainstorm—and remember that they are out in the open and
without shelter—and find them as dry as though they were

wearing raincoats. The wings are so tightly pressed together that the rain cannot find a way through. It is a good thing, too, for think what would happen to the lovely blue of the wings if the rain did creep in through the folds.

Watching the butterflies, and rejoicing in the sun and the breeze, I became conscious of some commotion on the part of the rooks. There were a pair of kestrels hovering above. I watched them for a moment or two, and they came lower and lower until they were poised only a couple of yards or so above the ground. Then the head would come down and the bird would dive the short distance to the grass and for a moment would be busy and then rise again to a considerable height before coming down once more to hover close to the ground. They were hunting grasshoppers— the grass was full of them. And the rooks were pestering the kestrels when they were on the ground by rising above them and swooping down with hoarse caws. It seemed as though the rooks wished to drive the kestrels away from the down. It was exciting to watch. The kestrels did not want to go from so sweet and easily-obtained a meal. They ignored the rooks, and the rooks became more persistent. They swooped lower and lower on the feeding falcon, until just when a collision seemed inevitable the kestrel would crouch close to the ground and the rook would go sailing over it. Then the kestrel would rise and soar above the rook, and find a convenient current of air, and commence hovering again. But the rooks won. They pressed their attacks and, in the end, the kestrels found it impossible to keep their attention on the grasshoppers and the rooks. They soared upward and the rooks followed, but always the kestrels kept the higher position and the rooks could not get at them. But still the kestrels were driven off over the edge of the Down, and shortly the rooks came back and settled down to work upon the grasshoppers themselves.

Soon the ground begins to fall away towards the valley of the Kennet, a green undulating tree-laden valley it seems from this height. The undulations hide Avebury, but the great mound of Silbury is immediately visible. From up here it looks little more than a pimple on the face of the valley, but it is in fact the largest artificial mound in western Europe —in all Europe, for all I know—and it remains a mystery still. The track runs down to the Kennet by the village of East Kennet, joining the hard road just short of the village itself, and then on to the river. All this is about a mile to the eastward of Silbury Hill and perhaps a mile and a half to the south-eastward of Avebury. One would have thought that Avebury and Silbury and the Kennet Long Barrows would have had some influence on the course of the Ridge-way. Avebury is the centre of all this region, and you get to think of it as the centre of the Ridgeway too. But the track passes a good mile to the eastward of the village at its closest point, a branch track leading to the stones. It seems evident, therefore, that the road was in existence before the circle was erected, and that it followed the course it did because the river is most easily fordable just by the village of East Kennet.

I crossed the river—there is a bridge now—and came to the Great West Road and the lorries and the smell of petrol and oil, which struck my nostrils quite viciously after the miles of clean air on the Downs. This is the old Roman road from London to Bath, and it is noticeable how it does a little bend to curve round Silbury Hill. The Roman engineers were not always so careful, having a passion for the straight line, and this indicates, I like to think, that there was still in their day a pretty powerful taboo on Silbury, one which even they did not dare to offend. And so I came to Silbury, towering above me. It stands in a small circular hollow, and it is one hundred and thirty feet high. That perhaps does not give a true picture of its size. Perhaps it would be better to say that its base covers five acres. But that does not convey much more, for so few people have any idea how large an acre is. Perhaps it would be better to point out that Stonehenge could be comfortably accommodated on the top of Silbury Hill. That does give an idea of its immensity. But why this huge monument was built is still unknown, and I think likely to remain so. It looks like an enormous barrow, such as might have been built over the body of some great chieftain of the Early Bronze Age, but a shaft was sunk from the top in the eighteenth century and a tunnel was driven through in the nineteenth century and there has been some trenching done quite recently, and all this work has led to the discovery of practically nothing. Why all that work was put into it remains a mystery. It has been suggested that it was built as a great shadow hill to mark the path of the sun, but I do not think that that idea appeals to the archæologists and it does seem to be an excessive labour to achieve something that could be achieved so much more easily. It must, I think, have been something more than that. The one thing quite certain about Silbury is that it was built at the command of overwhelming impulse.

Rather less than a mile to the north of Silbury lies the village of Avebury. You can climb up over the shoulder of Waden Hill—and there is a pleasant view from the top that makes it well worth while—and get to the village that way, but I walked back to West Kennet, because I wanted to walk up the Stone Avenue. The road is hard tarmac, a main road—it has to be to carry the charabanc traffic at week-ends—and the Stone Avenue runs parallel in a field to one side. The stones, of course, are small modern ones for the most part, put up to indicate where the original ones stood. It is nice to know, but I must say that I always find them singularly unimpressive, not because of their lack of size but because of their lack of atmosphere. They have an impersonal civil-service look about them, no warmth. Avebury itself is very different. All the reconstruction in the world could not take the atmosphere from this place.

Avebury lies in an open, highly cultivated plain, with the bare Downs heaving gently upward into solitude on every side. Except in the immediate neighbourhood of the village itself there are hardly any trees, though when you look at the village from a distance, from the top of one of the surrounding Downs it does give the impression of being quite heavily wooded. I think myself that the trees in the village accentuate the feeling of solitude, the feeling of an oasis tucked away in a vast empty plain, and so you arrive in the right frame of mind.

And how well this place was sited! Avebury is situated at the very hub of the chalk lands and the high lands generally. From it men could walk on the high land westwards to the Mendips and northward to the Cotswolds, and from the Mendips west into Wales and from the Cotswolds north into Derbyshire and thus, on the high ridge of the Pennines, to Scotland and the high cold hills of the distant north. From Avebury men could walk the chalk hills through Berkshire and over the Chilterns and along the Downs that divide the Cambridgeshire fens from what was once thick forest land. It was along the Icknield Way that flints and men came from the great mines of Grime's Graves to Avebury, and it was from Avebury that men could walk the high tracks to the south-west and south, and so down into Cornwall on the one hand or by the highlands of Hampshire to the ridge of the North Downs and distant Kent, to the ridge of the South Downs and the coast of Sussex.

There could have been no place better suited for the building of a great temple. And that is what Avebury was, a great temple, the greatest temple of its sort in all Europe. You have got to get used to it a bit, of course—it does not smack against the eye as Stonehenge does—and on a fleeting visit it is not too easy to grasp the whole magnificence and grandeur of the place. And, of course, there is not so much of it left as once there was. William Stukely wrote in his *Abury* in 1743 that it showed " a notorious grandeur of taste, a justness of plan, an apparent symmetry, and a sufficient niceness in the execution: in compass very extensive, in effect magnificent and agreeable. The boldness of the imagination we cannot sufficiently admire ". It has suffered a good deal since then, and, though much excellent work has been done on it recently and the old stones have regained much of their former dignity, the present Avebury is but a damaged skeleton of the old.

Originally it must have been terrific, awe-inspiring in its grandeur. You can see that by the great encircling bank,

which is virtually intact except for the short stretch on the
north-west which has been levelled for farm buildings.
You can walk almost all round the whole circumference—it
is 4,400 feet round and it encloses 28½ acres—and as you
do so it becomes more and more marvellous that man should
ever have done this work at all, let alone with primitive
implements or no implements at all, and then you imagine
the stone circles within, knowing quite well that imagination
cannot do justice to what was once there, and you are awed.
That bank alone is enough to make you feel small and help-
less. Inside it there is a ditch cut in the chalk, a wide flat-
bottomed ditch, and the bottom of the ditch is no less than
fifty feet below the top of the bank. Heaven knows what
that work must have meant in terms of human labour and
social organization! The men that did it had no more than
antler " picks " and shoulder-blade shovels, and probably
much of the work was done with the bare hands. No doubt
they had some form of basket to carry away to the bank as
it got higher and higher the chalk displaced from the ditch,
and possibly they had a simple form of hoisting-tackle.
But they would not have had more than that, and that is
not the sort of tackle that a modern British workman would
do much work with. Yet they carved out of the chalk this
great ditch and built up this huge bank, and within this
great earthwork they raised circles of stones weighing many
tons apiece. There were two pairs of concentric circles of
enormous stones standing side by side within a single stone
circle (which is the largest of its kind in Europe) when the
temple had attained its final form.

But that was not the whole design. There was the
avenue leading southwards to the Kennet river and then
on to Overton Hill where it ended in another stone circle,
known as the Sanctuary. The avenue was made of paired
stones, alternately tall and slender and short and thick, and
I believe that some archæologists think that these were male
and female symbols. This avenue came through the bank
to the circles. Actually there are four entrances breaching
the bank, three of which at any rate are original, so there

ALONG THE
EASTERN ARM.
THE AVON AT
MANNINGFORD
ABBAS MILL

THE AVON AT
ENFORD

may once have been much more outside the encircling embankment than is visible to-day.

Stukely, indeed, says there was. Stukely was a great antiquarian—there can be no doubt about that. To begin with, at any rate, he was a most careful observer and a most careful recorder of what he saw. He says that there was another avenue of stones running out in a curve in the direction of Beckhampton. There is no sign of such an avenue to-day, and its existence at any time is, I believe, discounted by modern archæologists. It is quite true that Stukely did become rather romantic as he grew older, and that he saw in the whole plan of Avebury the symbol of a snake. The Beckhampton Avenue was the tail, the Kennet Avenue the neck, and the Sanctuary the head. You cannot see anything symbolic of a serpent to-day—and maybe there never was, save in Stukely's imagination—but there are two stones on the route of the supposed Beckhampton Avenue, which are popularly known as Adam and Eve and were called the Longstones Cove by Stukely, so it may be that he was putting down what he actually saw and not what he imagined he had seen. And at least there is no doubt about the Kennet Avenue. But quite likely he was imagining things. It is difficult not to do so at Avebury. It is difficult not to imagine that great bank lined with spectators or worshippers or whatever they may have been; difficult not to imagine priests within the stone circles and magical rites in the moonlight; easy to imagine human sacrifices. And if it is easy to imagine such things in this grim mechanized twentieth century, in this cynical debunking age, you cannot blame Stukely for imagining a serpent symbol in the romantic eighteenth.

All the same I do not think that it ever had anything to do with a serpent. But it did have a good deal to do with the sun. It may not be that the builders worshipped the sun : the whole thing may have been quite different and the sun used only to fix the time of certain festivals. But, though I am no archæologist, I rather doubt that. The place must have taken years and years to build anyhow. Even

D

though all the stone is local—it is sarsen, which is a siliceous
sandstone that must have been quite common in the form of
isolated boulders on these Wiltshire Downs at one time—
and even though they were not worked to any great degree,
but just dressed a little, even though no attempt was made
to match them for size, it still must have taken years and
years to build. And it would have taken years and years
longer if they had really had to worry about the position of
the sun at certain times. You could do that sort of thing in
Egypt without much trouble and without much waste of time,
but the sun is not quite so regular and constant in its appearance here, and there would inevitably have been a severe
time-lag, getting the sun fixed and then the stones fixed to
the position of the sun. That might have been done at
Stonehenge—there was more time—but there was not all that
time available here at Avebury. It is an early Bronze Age
building. The date of the final building, the completed
temple, has been fixed by the archæologists within the comparatively narrow limits of 1900 and 1800 B.C. But the date
for the original Avebury is not known. It must have been
a good while before that—right at the very beginning of the
Bronze Age—and the Bronze Age did not start much, if at all,
before 1900 B.C. So I fancy the place must have been a
temple for some form of sun worship.

That would have been a new form of religion for Britain.
The Stone Age peoples did not worship the sun. The
Neolithic people, who lived in the big trenched settlement
on Windmill Hill a little to the north-west looking down
on Avebury, a pastoral community tending flocks and herds
and using flint implements, worshipped the earth, if they
worshipped anything at all—the earth and the womb. They
must have witnessed the building of this temple, and the
coming of new Gods, with wonderment and awe, for the
Gods that could command so great an effort must have been
great Gods indeed. The Windmill Hill people (incidentally
what clumsy names the archæologists choose for these ancient
peoples—Windmill Hill people, Beaker-folk, Battle-axe folk,
Peterborough people, Urn folk, Food-vessel people, and so

40

on—if they were one-tenth as clumsy with their spades there would be no archæology at all : I often wonder what they christen their children) had nothing to do with the planning of Avebury, of course—that would have been beyond them—but they may well have had a great deal to do with the building of it. The Beaker-folk, who planned it, were conquerors from the Continent, but the Neolithic peoples of Britain were not wiped out any more than the Stone Age died a sudden death with the introduction of Bronze. It was probably the Neolithic population that provided the major part of the labour force needed.

Now, despite much good work, Avebury is but a skeleton. Stukely complains of the " wretched ignorance and avarice " that caused its destruction. The stones were brought down and incorporated in the little village and for the making of roads by the local inhabitants. Stukely tells us how it was done. " The method is to dig a pit by the side of the stone, till it falls down, then to burn many loads of straw under it. They draw lines of water along it when heated, and then with smart strokes of a great sledge-hammer, its prodigious bulk is divided into lesser parts." And so Avebury went. " Wretched ignorance and avarice." It is easy to say that when you happen to be an antiquarian and a rich man. It is easy for us, now, to regret the destruction and to blame the villagers that caused it. Everyone must regret the destruction of what was the largest work of its kind in Europe, but I cannot blame the villagers that carried out the demolition. No one had troubled to educate them to a proper appreciation of ancient monuments, no one troubled to see that they were properly housed, no one troubled to make them roads, and here was the material ready to hand. They showed, I think, a proper initiative under the circumstances. Divorced from them in time and circumstance, I regret what they did, but I do not blame them for doing just what I would have done had I been in their situation, just what, I suspect, Stukely would have done also.

Avebury village lies almost wholly within the circle of the great ditch and bank. Almost every house and wall and barn has something of sarsen stone in its make-up, and there is sarsen stone in many of the cottage paths. It would not be too much to say that the village of Avebury has been hewn out of the temple of Avebury. I do not find that unfitting. The temple was built in peace—there must have been a profound peace over all the countryside throughout the years of its building—and it was destroyed to make habitations for men and women as close to the soil as those ancient people who lived in the ditches of the trenched camp on Windmill Hill, men and women who led lives as pastoral, and in whose veins no doubt ran some of the blood of the builders.

The church stands just outside the rampart. And that, I think, is because there was a church here before ever there was a village, a little Saxon church built of chalk and sarsen stone, which was put up, it is said, by some Saxon king for the use of the shepherds. There was no manor here, and the Saxon church is noted in Domesday as being *in terra regis*. In Norman times it was made a cell of a French monastery, and this has led to the most remarkable thing in it—the font. Not all the Saxon work has disappeared, though there has been much restoration. I have read somewhere that the building has " suffered " much from restoration in the nineteenth century. I must admit that I do not like the nave arcade or the chancel—both works of the nineteenth century—but the fact remains that there would be no church here at all, nothing but a ruin, were it not for the restorers. And in any case there is still some work of Saxon date visible. The framework of the nave is certainly so, and so are the windows at the west end. But the remarkable thing about Avebury church—other than its width which seems to be out of all proportion to its length—is the font. I do not know if it is Saxon or Norman. It is certainly Saxon in character, but I understand that some authorities maintain that it is Norman in date. The sculpture on it is certainly Norman, and I should have said that the font was there when the monks from France took over, and that they set about bringing it up to date. The carving shows a bishop with his crozier, in vestments and mitred, and with a book in his hand. On the other side there is a dragon pulling at his vestments. It is a sculpture with a pleasant double meaning, I think, like so many of the sculptures and carvings done by the early craftsmen.

I wandered into the inn. Here you find no conversation about antiquities. Here the conversation in slow deep Wiltshire is about racehorses and jockeys. One of the great training stables of England is but a pace down the road, and horses are almost a religion in this neighbourhood. And every man is an authority and a judge of horseflesh and jockeyship. No matter how many Tudor Minstrels let them down, their knowledge and their judgment remain unquestioned, and if the conversation about horses becomes embarrassing there is always Gordon Richards—a local boy as near as makes no difference—to talk about and he is a safe subject.

In the bar were two American girls, sipping beer with a look of courageous distaste and listening to the horsey talk with amused bewilderment. They eyed my rucksack and my perspiration with even greater amusement, and shortly came over and sat beside me, and asked me where I had come from and where I was going and endless questions about Avebury, which I did my best to answer accurately. They were cycling round England for a holiday, and staying the night in a cottage in the village. Where was I sleeping? I did not know, but I had thought that the ditch did not look too bad a spot. And where was I eating? Again I did not know. And so we talked and talked and in the end I had dinner with them—and they insisted on paying for it, myself paying for the drinks—and then they came to see where I would choose to sleep.

In the half light the great stones looked gigantic, and strangely alive. The ditch looked twice as deep as in the daylight. Imagination could play some queer tricks in that light, and the smallest sound could be magnified to a threat. They did not like it at all. They watched me get down into the ditch, standing on the brim holding each other by

the hand, and when I was settled called that they would come and look for me in the morning, if I was still there, and I called back that I would teach them how to make coffee. They would not sleep there, down in that ditch, for all the dollars in Wall Street, they called, and departed quickly to the warmth and light of a cottage.

It was a ghostly place to sleep, and I cannot say that I was unaware of it. But it was sheltered and quiet, and I was tired. I saw no ghosts, and quickly dropped to sleep to the hooting of a tawny owl quite close by and the more distant long-drawn-out melancholy, but musical, crying of a long-eared owl. I woke early to the song of the lark, but I could not see the bird for the early mist lying thick close to the ground. Damp and rather cold it was. I walked down to the little stream and washed and shaved, and brought water back for my coffee. But I had had my breakfast before the two girls appeared, looking as fresh as though they had just stepped out of a beauty parlour. I got some more water and made them coffee too—too strong for them it was—and we made arrangements to meet in Christchurch a week from that day. By that time, they said, they would have sleeping bags and be hardened to sleeping out. I doubted it. I was halfway down the road to West Kennet when they passed me—a lift-girl and a manicurist from Brooklyn riding bicycles round England for fun.

The mist vanished early. It was going to be a hot day, and I had time and distance to make up, for I was far from the Avon and later on the road, due to the charming company I had been keeping, than I would normally have been. But climbing the Ridgeway again from East Kennet, I turned to look back on the ground that had seen the first real civilization in Britain. Not that Neolithic man was not civilized in some measure. He had his flocks and his herds, his settlements and his tracks, his trade in flints and his mines and his miners. But how far behind the men who conceived Avebury was he ! This undoubtedly was the first real civilization in Britain. And all around me were the signs of it and of the men who had lived on these chalk hills in the dim past. Men live and work here to-day, cars race down the road that the Romans built, aeroplanes are ever present above the larks, but this is the country of the dead, and the wind whispering in the grasses, my feet brushing against the bents, say " shush, shush ", imploring silence for the spirits of the dead, who lie in this chalk, beneath these humped graves that we call barrows.

I went back the way I had come, along the Ridgeway, and I walked fast until the track joined the road. There I crossed to Knap Hill and stood on the ancient embankment and looked back and around at the long bare lines of close turf, flung high to the sky. Whatever else has changed in England these hills remain the same as when man first was buried here. Modern man may drive his road across them, may fence them here and there, may scratch the thin soil above the chalk to conjure a crop in emergency, but alter them he cannot. A road has been driven across them from Alton Barnes to East Kennet. It cuts the hills, ignoring the flow of the chalk, as though determined to impose its will upon them. Scarcely a soul lives by it. It seems small and lost and forlorn, frightened, deserted by those for whom it was made, ill-cared for. The hills sweep up around it, engulfing it, and it clings to them despairingly. A bare half-mile to the west the Ridgeway also clings to the hills, but as a child to the breast, drawing continual strength from them. With that strength, obedient to the parent, following the lines ordained for it, it swings gloriously on, broad and majestic. Even the trees ram home the lesson. There are not many, but here and there, looking away to the blue distance, you see the black plum-pudding tumps of hill-top beeches. Attractive they are undoubtedly, but in this immensity they appear lost, unnatural, quite unlike the long hangars of Hampshire, the thick caterpillars that fall down the hills of Sussex, for they again fall to the flow of the chalk ; these are imposed upon it.

Honey Street lies a quarter of a mile beyond Alton Barnes. The road to Woodborough crosses the canal here, and there is a timber wharf around which a few cottages have sprung up. After the silence and loneliness of the Ridgeway and the Downs the whine of the saws, the puffing of a small engine, the sudden clatter of a lorry, seemed almost deafening. Surprising to me, too, for when last I was here the wharf was silent and had been silent for some years. Great business had been done here in the First German War, and then with the cessation of hostilities had come cessation of business. Weeds grew in the yards, the sheds decayed, barges ceased to use the canal and it was only infrequently that it was dredged. It would be wrong to say that Honey Street was derelict between the wars, but it was very near to it. And now it was literally humming with activity. The yard was clean, the sheds repaired and on the canal there was a barge. Lorries were loading timber. The little cottage by the bridge was bright with flowers and new paint and the old farmhouse had a tended garden.

An old man leant on the bridge watching all this, and I joined him, as interested as he.

" How long has all this been going on ? "

" Couple o' year," he said ; " new people."

He did not speak quite like a Wiltshireman. It was Wiltshire dialect all right, but rather quicker in delivery than is normal for a Wiltshireman and with a clipped ending to the sentences that would be beyond the power of any Wiltshire countryman to produce.

" You're not a native hereabouts, are you ? " I asked.

" Born and bred in Barnes," he said, " and lived here all my seventy-eight years. That's native enough, I reckon, guv'nor."

" It is, indeed," I acknowledged, " but, you know, you don't speak quite like a Wiltshireman. That's why I asked."

" Ah "—he took a long pull at his pipe, let the smoke through his nose, spat into the canal, and looked at me—" ah, fancy you noticing that, now. Fancy. You'll find a few of us up and down the canal, folk like me, that speak a bit different like. My mother now, she came from Pewsey, and my grandmother, she came from Devizes. I reckon it's all along o' my grandfather. He came from Yorkshire,

'Alifax it was, and he worked on the canal, the building of it."

" But that was a long time ago. Eighteen hundred and one or thereabouts, wasn't it ? I should not have thought that you would have kept any of his talk."

" Never saw 'im, I didn't. But father, 'e spoke like I do, so I reckon it must have been on account of grandfather. You'll find chaps along this canal with Irish names—O'Connor and Murphy and such like—and that goes back to the building too, and they speak a bit different I'm told. There was a schoolmaster here once, and 'e were very interested in it, and took down a lot of names, and that. Going to put it in the papers, 'e said. But I never saw."

Great numbers of men must have invaded this quiet Vale when the canal was being built. The wages were good, for those days, and advertisements were put in the country papers all over England for workers. Most of the labour was Irish or Scots or Welsh, and as is the way of invaders the world over, they made pretty free with the local women. Some stayed and settled down, but most left when the work was done, though few can have gone without leaving their mark. Rough hard men they were, as accounts in the local papers of the day make only too plain. There were fights with the local villagers and men died, but besides a canal and trade, new blood was also brought into the countryside, and that was to the good. It is a curious thing that these great invasions of the English countryside should all be connected with transport—the building of canals and railways in peace-time, and during the last war with the building of great aerodromes. Each invasion brings its frictions with the local inhabitants, and each invasion brings in new blood. In the past the local blood has reasserted itself in course of time—as indeed it will do after conquest—but I am not sure that that will ever happen again. Transport is too quick now-adays, the world has shrunk ; and the language of the films is replacing dialect everywhere. Wiltshire is already speaking with the tongue, if not yet with the intonation, of The Bowery. I regret the ever-quickening disappearance of dialect (I would like to see it encouraged in rural schools—a hopeless wish in these days of standardization—for it has vigour and personality, things which are singularly lacking in modern civil-service English) but I do not regret the introduction of new blood into these country villages. There are villages in Wiltshire (as there are in Dorset) in which every single person bears a strong family resemblance to every other one—so much so that you are surprised to hear that So-and-So is only a cousin of Such-and-Such. So, even if it is not always achieved in a manner likely to win the approval of the Vicar, the introduction of new blood brought about by these transport invasions is a very good thing since it revitalizes a population inherently and economically addicted to inbreeding. The supreme importance of the cross in human breeding is not sufficiently realized. Without it, you get no brilliance. It has been said often enough (and it is true) that there has never been a brilliant Englishman. It is the crossing of good stocks that produces brilliance. The crossing of English (Anglo-Saxon would, I suppose, be a better term) with Welsh that produced Shakespeare and Cromwell; of English and Irish that produced Wellington; of British and American that produced Winston Churchill. Look up the parentage of a brilliant man and you will find a cross. It is the fantastic admixture of bloods in the Cockney that has made him so proverbially quick in the up-take. It is the almost unbelievable purity in the blood of the Wiltshire villager that makes him so slow of speech and movement.

It might be thought that this is advocating a polyglot race. Far from it. The basic strains survive throughout the years no matter what amount of crossing there has been. Crossing revitalizes : it does not extinguish. Neolithic man was short and dark with a neat long head. The type is common in the west to this day—the physical strain has survived—and is often (mistakenly) called " Celtic ". Bronze Age man and Celt and Roman and Saxon and Norman have come since, and overrun the country, and swamped the culture existing at the time, but that early physical strain survived. The Beaker-folk still exist as a physical type—you can find them in Wales too—and the tall, strong-jawed, fair-haired Celt has also survived Saxon and Norman. These physical strains have survived despite constant inter-marriage. It has always been the custom of conquerors and settlers to help themselves to the land *and* the women. Crossing does not extinguish, but it does bring in new life and new vitality.

Whoever it was designed this canal was an artist of genius. It lies on the very edge of the Vale, keeping as close under the Downs as the slope of the hills will allow, curving where they curve, the bank on the hillside being in many cases the actual rise of the hill from the Vale. The bank on the other side has the towing path, and in places there is a drop from the path to the fields of some ten feet or so. Thus, the canal has the appearance of being on the very rim of the Downs where they meet the Vale. And, since it curves with the curves of the Downs, it does not seem at all like a man-made waterway, but rather like a very sluggish river. Even the banks on this stretch do not look like the banks of a canal. Nature in almost one hundred and fifty years has done much to hide the hard lines, and disuse has done the rest. Thorns and briers and bramble, and all the tangle of convolvulus and bryony and nettles, have clothed the nakedness of the banks —sometimes in great hedges and sometimes in large clusters —and reeds and flags have conquered at least a yard of water from each bank, so that even more it has the appearance of a river. From Honey Street eastwards through the Vale the canal is little used now, and great fronds of water-plants, inextricably intertwined, almost fill the channel. Persicaria and arrowhead grow among the reeds and flags, and here and there are great stretches of duckweed, vividly green. The towpath, too, is fighting a losing battle with nature. Every now and then, as you walk, you see a brick or a stone and realize with something of a shock that once this path was paved throughout its length. Then it was broad and tramped by great horses ; now it is but a narrow strip between high undergrowth, a strip that survives only because a few fishermen and an occasional courting couple come this way.

Between Honey Street and Wilcot there are a number of high humped-back bridges—mostly farm bridges, though from one a rough lane leads to Woodborough and from another Cocklebury Lane runs to Wilcot, and some of them real works of art—and by each bridge there is a notice about the fishing belonging to some association. I saw no man fishing the length I walked from Honey Street to the farm bridge beyond Cocklebury, but I did see plenty of fish. The water was alive with them : perch, shoals of them, and roach and rudd (I put them both because I am not at all sure that I can tell the difference between them in the water when I am looking down on them from a bridge) and slim active bleak. You could not look into that water and not see fish. It seemed a pity about those notices.

All " coarse " fish. I often wonder where that term came from and what it means. It is a very unfortunate word. I suppose that it may have something to do with the eating value of the fish, for it is generally agreed that the salmon and the trout make better eating than the pike and the tench. But a good deal of that depends on the cooking—pike is an excellent dish if you know how to cook it. It can have nothing to do with the catching of them. The man who pays £1,000 or more for a stretch of chalk stream, who pays all that for a couple of months on a salmon river, may look at the coarse fishes with contempt ; the dry-fly purists may regard with contempt the humble fisherman by Thames side ; too often they do : but there can be no doubt whatever that it is the coarse fishes that provide the best and most artistic angling in the world. Furthermore, they provide the only cheap fishing that can be had in this country.

" The best and most artistic angling in the world." Yes, there is no doubt about that. Outwitting a coarse fish is a thousand times more difficult than outwitting a trout ; the salmon is a positive fool compared with the carp. I have never caught a carp, though I have tried. It is difficult business and one that few men deliberately undertake nowadays. There used to be in *The Field* office, immortalized in a glass case, a carp of some 16 lb. that had been caught by the late Hugh Sheringham, once Angling Editor of that paper. Sheringham may, therefore, be considered an expert on the Queen of the Rivers, as old Izaak Walton called the carp, and this is what he had to say about carp-fishing :

You cannot, of course, fish for a big carp in half a day. It takes a month. So subtle are these fishes that you have to proceed with the utmost precautions. In the first week, having made ready your tackle and plumbed the depth, you build yourself a wattled screen, behind which you may take cover. By the second week the fish should have grown accustomed to this, and you begin to throw in ground-bait composed of bread, bran, biscuits, peas, beans, strawberries, rice, pearl barley, aniseed cake, worms, gentles, bananas and potato. This ground-baiting must not be overdone. Half a pint on alternate evenings is as much as can safely be employed in this second week. With the third week less caution is necessary, because by now the carp will be less mindful of the adage concerning those who come bearing gifts. You may bear gifts daily, and the carp will, it is to be hoped, in a manner of speaking, look these gifts in the mouth—as carp should. Now, with the fourth week comes the critical time. All is very soon to be put to the touch.

On Monday you lean your rod (it is ready put up, you remember) on the wattled fence so that its top projects eighteen inches over the water. On Tuesday you creep up and push it gently, so that the eighteen inches are become four feet. The carp, we hope, simply think that it is a piece of the screen growing well, and take no alarm. On Wednesday, Thursday and Friday you employ the final and great ruse. This is to place your line (the depth has already been plumbed, of course) gently into the water, the bullet just touching the bottom so that the float cocks, and the two feet of gut which lie on the bottom beyond it terminating with a bait in which there is no fraudful hook. This is so that the carp may imagine that it is just a whim of the lavish person behind the screen (be

51

sure they know you are there all the time) to tie food to some fibrous yet innocuous substance. And at last, on Saturday, the 31st of the month, you fall to angling, while the morning mists are still disputing with the shades of night. Now there is a hook within the honey paste, and woe betide any carp which loses its head. But no carp does lose its head until the shades of night are disputing with the mists of evening. Then, from your post of observation (fifty yards behind the screen), you hear a click, click, which tells you that your reel revolves. A carp has made off with the bait, drawn out the five yards of line coiled carefully on the ground, and may now be struck. So you hasten up and strike. There is a monstrous pull at the rod point, something pursues a headlong course into the unknown depths . . .

Maybe it is as difficult as that. I would not know. But I have seen a carp caught on this canal—just beyond Cocklebury Bridge where there is a pool and it is wide—and it was the biggest carp I have ever seen, one that put that glass-cased specimen in *The Field* office to shame. It was in August, which is the month when the carp come to the surface to disport themselves with their ladies, and it was caught by a dog. The boys of the village were out for their Sunday afternoon walk—that walk that is common to village lads throughout the country—and watching the carp at their amusement when one put his dog, a cross-bred Labrador, into the water. To everyone's surprise he got his fish at the first plunge, but he was not strong enough to hold it and had to make many big sallies before he could drive the fish close enough into the bank for the boys to tail it. I saw it on the bank. It must have been three feet long. I could not weigh it, but it cannot have been far off 30 lb. in weight—a very good evening meal for one family in the village that night. Many times since that August have I watched the carp disporting themselves in these shallows, but never have I seen another caught.

I thought about that carp as I walked along the towpath,

and hoped that I would see another, but my mind was on the perch. This was the fish of my childhood—and I suspect yours—this was the fish I began on, the first fish I ever caught. Perhaps it is the first fish to all men, perhaps all men get the same thrill as I do whenever I see a perch, perhaps their minds go back as mine does to that first day, that first tremendous thrill as the float bobbed and I pulled hard and there on the hook kicked a striped green fish with a silver tummy and red fins. It was a very small one, I am sure, but it remains the perch of all perch to me.

The perch is gregarious. But he is careful of his company. As I strolled down the towpath I noticed how the perch in a shoal were all of the same size, the bigger the fish the smaller the shoal. He is a predatory fish and a swift swimmer, and if he were a little bigger he would be a menace indeed in any water. He thrives in this canal, but here, of course, the pike is the murderous fellow and some of the pike grow to great weights.

> Hist! there's a pike, see, nose against the river,
> Gaunt as a wolf, the grim, old privateer?

Austin Dobson must have been a fisherman, I think. But here, in this canal, the pike like to lie tail to bank, nose just peeping through the covering reeds, and to raid from there the unsuspecting fish or bird. And sometimes you may hear an agonized squawk and see a swirl in the water and know that one more moorhen has failed to cross from reeds to reeds. So far as fishing goes, it is my experience that the smaller the pike the better the fight he will put up. I have caught big pike in my day, and never one have I found that did much more than shake its head once or twice and then roll over to be pulled in. But, if big pike do not take much catching, they do take a deal of killing. My friend, the late Patrick Chalmers, used to show the scars on his thumb where a pike that should have been dead had taken grip. He lost a good deal of blood that afternoon. And I have had a pike snap at me in the boat minutes after I had thought that I had killed him stone dead. Pike fishing—for fish about eight pounds in weight—is some of the best fun in the world, and pike are very good to eat.

It has always astonished me that so few people know that. Much depends on the cooking, of course. Any fool can cook a salmon or a trout, and a decent dish will result. Cooking a pike is a different matter altogether. But first, a word on cleaning your fish, for pike must be cleaned well. When cleaning a fish you should have it on its back. It is surprising how many people do not take care to do this. But if you do not, there is always the risk of the gall bladder breaking away and that will ruin the taste of your dish. It is also a good thing to clean a fish as soon as possible. Even if you have to leave it overnight before cooking, it should not be left uncleaned. Clean it, but do not leave it to soak in water—a very common mistake—for soaking soon robs it of its natural flavour. Instead, rub it inside and out with salt and vinegar—a teaspoonful of each to each pound that the fish weighs—if you have never done that you will be astonished and pleased at the result, for if you have never done that you do not know how good a fish can taste. Yes, even so muddy a fish as a tench—though I have known men carry a bottle of vinegar with them, when tench fishing, so that immediately they have got their fish they can pour a little down its throat.

I suppose that the usual way to cook pike is to bake it. That is quite a job, but the result can be delicious. First of all you must scale the fish and then dry it carefully with a clean towel. Then you need a pound of beef suet and a pound of grated bread, and mix and season with salt, pepper and nutmeg ; work into this some shredded lemon peel and some thyme and some chopped anchovies and the yolk of eggs (three eggs to an eight-pound fish), and then squeeze lemon juice over the whole, and place it in the stomach of the fish. Sew the fish up, and bake in an oven until the skin cracks. And now you need a sauce. This sauce is the real secret of baked pike. And the best sauce is compounded thus : a pint of beef gravy, a pint of skinned shrimps, half a pint of stewed mushrooms, a quart of stewed oysters, a wineglass full of

ABOVE FIGHEL-
DEAN. LOOK-
ING TOWARDS
NETHERAVON

THE AVON AT
FIGHELDEAN

port ; mix this into a pound of melted butter. Now take the thread out of your pike, pour the sauce over him, and enjoy yourself. Even if you do not like pike, you will enjoy that sauce—and there is no reason at all why you should not take it separately. Yes, I know that that is not a dish for these days of austerity. But it is worth remembering, just in case they ever end.

But there are ways of cooking pike that can be managed even in these days. The simplest (with a small fish) is this : clean your fish, but do not scale it. Rub it inside and out with salt and vinegar : bend it head to tail and fix it so with a wooden skewer : place it, back upwards, in just sufficient water to cover it, and boil slowly for half an hour. But the best way of all, in my opinion, to cook pike is this : Clean and scale your fish, and then boil or parboil it and then bone it : cut the white flakes of flesh into strips of an inch or so, and fry them in bread crumbs (if you have an egg so much the better). That served hot (with a lemon if possible) and thin bread and butter is a dish for a king.

But pike are, unfortunately, rather outside the scope of the walker : not an easy fish to cook over a wayside fire. On the other hand, you can catch your pike and take it to a cottage, and teach the housewife how to cook it the way you like and then share it with her and her family. That has been done before now—and not only with pike—and there are not many cottages that will not welcome the traveller that brings his own food with him. Even so, pike are, on the whole, best left alone by the walker ; not so perch. He is very easy to catch and he is very good eating indeed, rather bony, perhaps, but the equal in flavour of a brown trout. And he may be dealt with just in the same manner as a trout over a wood fire.

So, thinking a little of the good pike I have eaten and of the perch I might eat, I strolled leisurely along the towpath, first on the Vale side of the canal and then on the Down side. It was some time before I realized that there was something missing from the old days when I walked this canal. Then you could scarcely move a hundred yards without putting up

a heron. It was good fun stalking them. They were not at
all easy to see, for the reeds and flags among which they
stood were almost as tall as themselves and if they were out
of the reeds, then the banks, taller than they, would hide
them. The birds, of course, always saw me before I saw
them, but they would not move until almost the last moment,
only when they were convinced that I was going to walk
on to them. Then they would rise and flap slowly away,
describing a half-circle and settling in a field behind me,
standing straight and motionless until convinced that I was
out of range, and then they would flap back to their fishing.
In those days I used to carry glasses—I was not then walking
a distance, but just for a day—and it was fun to search the
reeds and pick out the fine grey head just topping the reeds,
and to know that the bird was unaware of you. It was fun
to stalk the bird, matching your skill in seeking cover against
the quickness of the bird's eye, fun trying to get into a
position in which you could see the whole of the bird without
the aid of glasses. It was herons on the banks of this canal
that taught me much of what I know of the art of getting
close to wild creatures without disturbing them. And once,
close by Cocklebury Bridge, I spotted a heron and stalked it,
and got close, and poked my head through a gap in the tall
grasses lining the bank and disturbed four herons together
—and that was the only time that I have seen herons really
move quickly from the take-off and the only time that I have
heard herons croak at the take-off.

But, normally of course, nothing like that happened. I
would spot a heron a good distance away and begin my
stalk. If I was kept to the towpath, as sometimes happened,
there was no point in crawling and the art was to walk as
slowly as possible, so that it did not appear that one was
moving towards the bird, stopping after each step or so.
Even that was not too easy, because of the moorhens that
would shoot from under the bank beside me and fly diagon-
ally forward across the canal with feet trailing noisily in the
water until they tumbled into the reeds on the other side.
They were warning enough for any heron, but the bird would

take no notice until I was about fifty yards away. Then the head would come round, and I would get that very odd sensation of being watched by the piercing eyes of a large bird. Once the head was round it was no good going on with the stalk. I could stand as still as stone, but that would be no good. After a moment or two, just the few seconds needed by the heron to take a really good look, the bird would rise and flap slowly away. Usually there would be that half-circle and it would land in the middle of a field behind me. In that position it would not be many yards further from me than it had been on the canal when it got up, but it would be quite satisfied with this new position, seeming to forget at once that it was this human being, staring at it now, that had disturbed its fishing but a moment or two before. When they landed in the fields like this, they would always preen themselves—the breast feathers first— and then they would stretch their wings, relaxing and drooping them until the tips almost touched the ground. Then they would rest head upon shoulders, beak along the doubled neck, and apparently go to sleep. Perhaps they would stand thus for ten minutes. But if I stayed too, its patience would be spent and it would walk with dignity across the field and hide itself behind a bush or in a fold in the ground. Herons walk with a ridiculous dainty dignity, stepping high and with deliberation, the head bobbing forward with each step— ridiculous indeed it would look were it not for the real beauty of the grey plumage. Sometimes, when a heron had thus walked behind a bush to hide itself, I would walk along until I could again get a view of it. There it would be standing, in just the same position as before apparently asleep. But this time there would be no ten-minute wait. Almost at once it would forsake that hunched-up attitude : the wings would be drawn in close to the body, the neck would shoot up to its full length and height, the head would be turned towards me, suspicious and alert—that damned fellow again —and then, in a moment, there would be a heron flapping slowly out of sight across the canal.

And now there were no herons. Not one did I see in

the whole length from Honey Street to Cocklebury. There
was a heronry near by in the old days, and now, obviously,
it was deserted. In the big reed bed in the Broadwater by
Cocklebury Bridge a pair used to nest on the ground (reverting
to what must once have been the habit of all herons, for those
long legs were never made for perching in trees), sharing
the reeds with a pair of swans—a sufficiently extraordinary
proceeding. The swans were still about, and four cygnets
too, but never a heron in the whole length. That terribly
hard winter must have reduced the heron population of
Britain drastically, and I suppose that it will be years and
years before this canal again has a heron along every reach.
But I did see a kingfisher, just the flash beneath Cocklebury
Bridge, and that is a bird that I do not see so often now as I
did, say, twenty years ago. It is not a succession of hard
winters that has reduced the kingfisher population. It is
man's horrible habit of polluting his rivers.

Beneath Cocklebury Bridge there was a small motor-
launch moored. A girl was brewing something on a small
stove. She looked up as I approached and sang out, " Good
morning." I sat down on the bank above her and lit my
pipe.

" Come far ? " she asked.

" Only from Avebury this morning. And you ? "

" From Bristol, but by degrees. We did not move at all
yesterday, this is such a nice place, and I love that little hill."
She cocked a hand towards Picked Hill, rising like a pyramid
just behind me. It is an outlier of the great Downs behind,
a steep triangular hill of almost seven hundred feet with a
single thorn tree growing in a hollow almost at the top.
The walk up one side is easy enough, a steepish slope, no
more ; but on the two others it is really steep so that you
have to scramble rather than walk. Many and many are the
days I have spent in the past lazing on Picked Hill, and I could
well understand what had made her spend a whole day
moored up below it.

" Um, so do I," I said ; " there's many the day I've spent
dozing up there. Where are you going on to ? "

" To Reading from here. And then up other canals into the Midlands, but I don't know just where or how. John'll know though. He'll be back in a minute—he's gone to get some milk."

And from the way she said " John "—and the trust in her voice that he would know—I knew that they were on their honeymoon. And then I could hear John singing in the lane on the other side of the bridge, and soon he appeared carrying a can of milk. He wore shorts and a bush shirt, a small dark man with a stubby briar pipe. He did not see me sitting on the bank, and sang out from the top of the bridge, " Kate. Kate, is dinner ready? I'm as hungry as hell." And the voice was rich, almost heavy, with the brogue of Donegal. Then he saw me ; " Ah, hullo," he said, " would you be wanting some food now? "

" I would that," I said. " I was hoping I'd be asked, but your wife was too shy."

" I thought you would have your own in that rucksack you've got," she said, " but we'd be pleased."

A good meal it was too, and good tea afterwards, and another pipe—he smoking my tobacco and I smoking his, and she a cigarette. " On your honeymoon, aren't you? "

The girl blushed delightfully, slowly from her neck to the roots of her hair (it always amazes me why girls should blush at the word honeymoon, since it is what they have spent a good deal of time to secure), but the man laughed and said, " Yes, we are. But how did you know? "

" Oh, the way Kate here said John, just before you came back with the milk. You never hear that tone of voice in a woman who's been married long."

They both laughed at that and said that they hoped they would prove me wrong in time (but they won't) and that I'd better come and see them in a couple of years. And on that we exchanged addresses, and maybe one day I will.

But what a honeymoon trip—to take a small motor-launch through the waterways of England, camping out all the way. That should be a good start to any marriage, I feel, for the girl that will do that, forsaking all the new dresses and new furniture and what-not that goes with a newly acquired husband (and is often I suspect more important than the new husband) is the right sort of companion to have in life surely. She had been in the A.T.S. and came from Coventry and knew nothing at all of country life till now.   He had been in Burma —the Duke of Wellington's—and was the son of a small farmer in Donegal.   And when this trip was over, they were going to farm a small-holding in the Donegal mountains.   A hard life that, if ever there was one—but grand and satisfying in the right company.   I wondered if the girl had any idea at all what she was in for.

Cocklebury Lane—and that is a strange name to find in the middle of Wiltshire—leads past some small-holdings and the high wall of the Manor garden to the village of Wilcot. In wet weather it can be the muddiest lane in England and it is much used by cattle from Maidment's Farm.   I went on down the canal path past the Broadwater to the next farm bridge—not because I wished to avoid the mud ; it was a dry day in any case—but because I wanted to see again the little cottage by the farm bridge.   Thatch has been much used in Wiltshire from the earliest times—from before the Celtic villages—until just the other day.   " Clunch ", which is the harder, deeper blocks of chalk, has been used for almost as long—from the ramparts of Iron Age townships to cottage walls of yesterday.   Sarsen stone made the early temples and dolmens and the passage ways of the long barrows, and then was used again for the walls of cottages and houses and even churches.   But Wiltshiremen also made bricks from the clay smears, and used nodules and nuggets of flint, and pudding stone in the building of their cottages.   Wilcot, though you will not find it mentioned in *The Highways and Byways* volume nor even marked on the map in that book, though it is not mentioned—so far as I am aware—by any writer on the county, is a most attractive little place and contains more and better thatch than any other village in Wiltshire.   Moreover, it is one of the few villages in England where thatching is still normally carried on, for it contains the best family of thatchers still working regularly in England (and you may

see their work with its unmistakable sign all over England,
down into Kent and up into Yorkshire). But of all the
thatched cottages of Wilcot there is none to compare with
this isolated little place by the canal side. It is not so beautiful
as some—there is one at the end of the village street, hard by
Wilcot Bridge, that is beyond compare—but it has all the
things that are really Wiltshire. A sarsen forms the corner
stone : the walls are blocked chalk : the lavatory down the
garden path is of flint and brick ; an outhouse of pudding
stone completes the picture, save for the thatch, which on the
canal-ward side falls almost to the ground. For years it was
deserted : isolated from the village with only a path across
the big field of Maidment's Farm as access : with the reputation of being damp so close to the canal, no one was going
to live in it. War brought a shortage of housing accommodation even in the heart of rural Wiltshire, and now it has been
taken over and done up—by " gentry ", I should say, from
the window decorations—and looks as snug and comfortable
as could be.

I went on down the canal past the village of Wilcot to the
long wooded reach by Stowell Park—a beautiful piece this,
with, as always, an assortment of duck up-ending in it.
Domestic duck these are, but it would defeat any naturalist to
name the breed. All of them have some mallard blood, and
the rest seems to be made up of Khaki Campbell and Indian
Runner and Aylesbury with perhaps a dash from somewhere
of Muscovy. So you see an apparently pure bred Khaki
Campbell with the wild duck speculum or a pure white
Aylesbury with the same. Many wild duck of many species
come to the lake in Wilcot Manor—mallard and tufted and
teal, an occasional wigeon even—and the mallard drake, like
the cock pheasant, is a bit of a Don Juan. But the nice
thing about these ducks of the canal is that they fly, if not
quite so well as a wild duck, at least well enough to make a
most satisfying sight. Beyond this stretch the towpath becomes rather dull, running below what used to be the golf
course of Pewsey and there is rather too much wire to make
walking comfortable. And so to Pewsey Wharf and the

little inn called the French Horn—a name that reminds one interested in history that here was one of the big prison camps of the Napoleonic Wars.

Pewsey in the time since I had last been here has changed hugely—I do not know that there had been much building —I saw a few new council cottages, but that was all—but in its amenities. There used to be a small cinema held in a hall above a shop ; now there is a new cinema by the bridge over the river. A milk-bar has blossomed (and a very good milk-bar too—not laid out on the normal plan—where I had a most excellent tea for one shilling and threepence) and the shops, that in my day had been no more than good village shops, had taken on something of the air of town shops without losing their village fronts. But the most noticeable difference was in the buses. Not many years ago there was scarcely a bus that thought it worth while visiting Pewsey. About twice a day there would be a bus to Salisbury, once a week one to Devizes, perhaps twice a week one to Marlborough. Now, there are bus-stop signs in the street, different stops for the different services, " Q this Side " notices, and all the paraphernalia of a regular town-bus service. And there are, in fact, almost half-hourly services to Salisbury and Marlborough and not much less frequently than that to Devizes. Pewsey has always been the capital of this little Vale. Now it is taking on the atmosphere of a capital.

Passing down the street from the milk-bar I noticed again the name Amor over a shop-front—a good chalk-country name, this ; not specifically Wiltshire, but specifically chalk, for you will find it in Hampshire and Sussex and Dorset on the chalk, and not much elsewhere—and was reminded again of Pewsey's murder story. It is not a very good murder story, but it has a good solution. About the year 1810 a man named Dyke was robbed and murdered one dark night on the road between Wilcot and Pewsey by a Pewsey man named Amor. It was a sordid affair done for a few pence. The murderer's footsteps were traced back to the village, but that was all. Nothing more could be made of it. But the Rector of Pewsey at that time, a man named Townsend,

was a man of resource. After Sunday service he com-
manded his congregation to remain, had the body of the
murdered man brought in, and then made every person in
the congregation lay his hand on the poor battered face and
looking at the altar say : " I swear, before Almighty God, I had
nothing to do with this horrid deed." People in those days
went to church, and the Rector must have been fairly certain
that if the murderer was a local man he would be in church
for the morning service, for it would have aroused comment
had he not been. Amor was in church, and when it came to
his turn to lay his hand on the face he could not face the ordeal.
He was searched and upon his person there was found the
watch of Mr. Dyke. He was hanged upon a gibbet raised in
the square just in front of the Phœnix inn.

History in the main has passed Pewsey by. But the church
is worth a visit, not so much for its architecture as because
it is a veritable museum of oddments. The nave is transitional
Norman, the chancel thirteenth century, the tower and the
aisles Perpendicular. The arcades of the nave are primitive
in the extreme, but the chancel with its sedilia and piscina
has quite definite charm. But the most interesting feature
architecturally is the woodwork. I do not think that there
was ever much money in Pewsey and the wood seems to have
been picked up as opportunity offered. The communion
rails, for instance, are ship's timbers. I forget which ship—
and I could not find anyone to tell me—but it was one of the
French vessels captured at Trafalgar. The wood of the
reredos, too, served some other purpose before it was carved
for this church. And so too with the roof of the organ
chamber and the vestry. At one time this formed part of the
very fine roof of Ivychurch Priory. At the Dissolution the
land and buildings of that Priory came into the possession of
the Dean and Chapter of Sarum. They leased the property
to the Earl of Pembroke, and at the beginning of the nineteenth century the Pembrokes sold it to the Earl of Radnor.
To begin with, the Earl of Radnor had the buildings converted
into a school, but later he had them pulled down with the
exception of part of the church. The wood was left lying

about until, in 1888, the then Rector of Pewsey begged them
from the then Earl and roofed his vestry and organ chamber
with them. As a picker-up of unconsidered trifles Pewsey
church must rank high.

Here, too, in a pillar of one of the columns of the nave,
shielded by glass, is one of the feathers of the Archangel
Gabriel. Presumably he lost it during a reconnaissance flight
over the neighbourhood. What bird it came from it is
impossible to say. The glass shields it from touch, and years
and years of dust have overlaid the colours. There are those
who maintain that it is the feather of a great bustard and it
is true that once the great bustard must have been common
on the Downs hard by. But I think it is highly improbable
that it is a bustard feather. It appears to have neither the
shape nor the texture that one would expect in the wing
feather of a bustard, and it is obviously a wing feather.
Personally, I am inclined to the belief that it is no more than
a wing feather from a domestic hen.

The only other thing of note about Pewsey is " Pewsey
Feast "—pronounced by old locals Pewsedge veast. Pewsedge, incidentally, is the ancient name of the village. I was
too early in the year for the feast, but I remember it as a
great local event with a procession—farm carts with tableaux,
bands and dancing, coconut shies and swings and so forth.
There was more than a little drinking that night, and perhaps
a fight or two, and a good deal of indiscriminate love-making,
and much jollity. All very reprehensible in some eyes, but
it did a lot of people a lot of good and I doubt if it did
anyone any permanent harm.

The river Avon runs through Pewsey, and now I was back
again on my route. It is a tiny stream here—you could call
it a prattling brook in the summer-time—but in some winters
it can become a river indeed, spilling over its banks and
flooding the town to no mean extent. Actually, the water
running through Pewsey itself is the Deane Brook (the Deane
Water on the Ordnance Survey Map) and it is joined on the
east of the village by the Easton Brook, which is itself joined
about halfway on its length by the Fifield Brook. The

Easton Brook, which rises at the foot of Easton Down crowned by an ancient earthwork, brings in quite a volume of water (the Fifield Brook is negligible in this respect) but the main stream comes from the Deane Brook. The Deane Brook flows through quiet agricultural country, avoiding all villages, and then curves eastwards to rise just beyond Congyre Farm and almost in the village of Burbage. It is a quite undistinguished little brook—though I was surprised to see in its upper reaches, beyond Tatteridge Farm, a quite sizeable trout—flowing softly through quite undistinguished country, but with the great bluff of Martinsell always on your left, towering over the Vale.

The Easton Brook flows past the village of Milton Lilbourne—the second part of the name is usually dropped as is the Royal from Easton Royal—and here the hills creep down again, closing in on the Vale and altering the whole character of the countryside. The church at Milton is small and so much restored that it has lost all character, but in the churchyard—I knew it though I could not find the grave—lies George Carter, who was huntsman to Assheton Smith, the famous master of the Tedworth. Assheton Smith was a character, an eccentric, a man of vast impetuosity, as everyone familiar with hunting literature will know, but his huntsman must have been as wild a man in his moments as his master. For it was George Carter who rode his horse and took his hounds down the steepest face of Martinsell, the while—so tradition says—his master rode round the soft way. And if you look at Martinsell from the Vale north of Pewsey, you will agree that for once in his life Assheton Smith chose the wiser course.

Easton Royal is deeper still into the hills. Its church was built by an ancestor of mine in the sixteenth century, and I am sorry to say that it is not worth a visit. But then he was a dull man anyway. This little village was a great Royalist stronghold, and it was here that two of the plots against Cromwell, after his successful rebellion, were hatched. Neither came to anything, but each caused the Dictator some moments of worry.

From Easton I climbed the steep hill, and continued over it until I saw the main road from Marlborough below me. This was a digression from the Avon, of course, but it had more justification than my previous one, for on this side of the wall of chalk lies the source of the Bourne River, which flows through the Collingbournes to join the main stream at Salisbury. In fact, as the crow flies, there is not more than a mile separating the source of the Easton Brook beyond Easton Royal and the source of the Bourne River at Marr Green, but the hill between is barrier enough for any but a man on foot or a man on horseback.

It was on horseback that Cobbett came here, and I followed in his steps. He came from Everleigh on the Marlborough road, and he must have come through the Collingbournes and then taken the track up the Downs opposite Aughton Farm. I came down on to the road and walked down it to that track and then turned as he must have done, and so I came to the high ground on which he stood and viewed the Valley for the first time.

At the end of about a mile [he wrote] from the top of a very high part of the down, with a steep slope towards the valley, I first saw the *Valley of the Avon*; and a most beautiful sight it was! Villages, hamlets, large farms, towers, steeples, fields, meadows, orchards, and very fine timber trees, scattered all over the valley. The shape of the thing is this : on each side *downs*, very lofty and steep in some places, and sloping miles back in other places ; but each *out-side* of the valley are downs. From the very edge of the downs begin capital *arable* fields, generally of very great dimensions, and, in some places, running a mile or two back into little *cross-valleys*, formed by hills of downs. After the corn fields come *meadows* on each side, down to the *brook* or *river*. The farm houses, mansions, villages, and hamlets are generally situated in that part of the arable land which comes nearest the meadows.

I stood where he stood and looked down on the same

scene—changed but little, I fancy, since his day, save for the distant smoke of an express on the main line to the south-west. I think it is true to say that in no other county of England do you get such a perfect view of the patchwork quilt as in Wiltshire—and this at any time of the year. In spring, it will be made up mainly of different shades of green: sea-green of wheat, black-green of clover, blue-green of oats, silver-green of barley, lush vivid green of the water-meadows, and the green of the trees—yellow, red, silver, emerald, of willow and poplars and larches—and here and there, to set it all off, the brown of a patch of fallow. In summer, different again: reds and yellows, golds and browns of wheat, silver of barley, platinum of oats, blue of rape, the burnt ochre of clover ripening in the sun, the green of the water-meadows, the blue-green of the roots, the fallow now chalky white. In winter, again different: greens and browns and greys and blues, it is true, but faded now, paler, and criss-crossed by black lines, the gaunt lines of hedgerows and trees.

But, yes, there was a difference; not only a difference from Cobbett's day, a difference from my own. The hedge-rows had been disciplined. In some places they had gone altogether, grubbed up by some gross machine. And with them had gone much of the special character of the place. Those lovely, huge, untidy hedgerows of Wiltshire! The birds they held and the butterflies and the moths! The wild flowers that grew by them, and the scents! The lovely aimless way they wandered over valley and hillside! Wire, no doubt, makes a better fence; a little more land has, no doubt, been secured for the planting of corn. But those lovely hedgerows had more than an æsthetic value: they had a most definite economic value, for they provided good shelter for both bird and beast (and sometimes for man also) and the birds now driven out were good friends in the war against insect pests. And what matter that, someone will say, in these days of D.D.T. and other lethal insecticides? We can get rid of the insects all right. "And what harm does D.D.T. and so forth do to the birds?" you ask. And,

immediately, post-haste, too anxiously, comes the answer :
" Oh, none at all." How dreadful is this materialistic inter-
ference with Nature, and how foolish ! If D.D.T. does all
the scientists claim for it—and there seems to be no doubt
that it does—then it is going very soon to make a sizeable
hole in the insect population. Presumably it is going to wipe
out large sections of it, if it is used thoroughly. D.D.T.
itself, it is true, is harmless to birds—but what are the insect-
eating birds going to live on when the insects have gone ?
And how is the insect population going to support with
greatly lessened numbers (supposing, as will be the case, that
it is not wiped out) the population of insect-eating and singing
birds ? The advertisers cannot have it both ways : if the
stuff is as good as all that with insects then it must definitely
harm the birds. " And suppose it does," say the materialists,
" what matter ? We shall get more food when the insect-
pests have been kept down or wiped out. D.D.T. is better
at the job than any number of birds." True enough, it is—
much better. But it is *not* selective. It kills both the pest
and the benefactor. Red spider is now becoming a menace
in orchards for just that reason.

Saddened by the disciplining of the hedgerows, and rather
chastened by my thoughts, I returned to Pewsey, and set
forth down the stream southwards.

For a mile or so the stream keeps company with the main
road. It is still little more than a brook, but there is now
more purpose in its current and it has begun to sing as it
runs. Just beyond the mill at Manningford Abbas it assumes
the proportions of a trout stream of some consideration.
There are three Manningfords—Abbas, Bruce and Bohune—
and the first two are actually off the course of the river by a
few hundred yards. The church at Manningford Abbas (that
was Abbots or Abbey once, of course) is not worth a visit.
It was completely rebuilt in about 1865, and is as dull as the
church at Easton. The church at Manningford Bohune was
rebuilt at about the same time and is if anything even more
disappointing. But that at Manningford Bruce demands a
visit and serious attention. Here is a complete pre-Conquest

church—the only other one in Wiltshire is that at Bradford-on-Avon (the other Avon) but this one has a semi-circular apse. It is not, however, as early as the church at Bradford, though I think that it is more interesting. It is bare and severe, without decoration either inside or out, its flint walls as firm to-day as when they were built. And it is built like a fortress, as though the builders and the worshippers were in constant fear of attack. There are very few windows, and such as there are are narrow and strategically placed, with wide splays on the inside and small rebates on the outside, which seem to have been designed to take shutters. There has, of course, been some restoration, but it has been most excellently and sympathetically done—so well done, in fact, that even the modern roof does not hit the eye. About its date there has been much argument. That it is later than the church at Bradford is obvious—a glance at the chancel arch is sufficient to show that—but that does not necessarily mean that it is not Saxon. The author of the *Highways and Byways* maintained that it is Norman work of Edward the Confessor's time, other authorities would give it a date in the tenth century. I am no authority myself on this sort of thing, but I must admit that I should not have thought that there was any Saxon of the tenth century capable of building that chancel arch. In any case, this is a very early church and I cannot see that at this date it is worth while quarrelling about fifty years or so; sufficient that it is a very early and very beautiful church.

One memorial within is of great interest. It is to the memory of one Mary Lane, who married Edward Nicholas of this parish and who died in 1686.

Underneath this lieth the body of Mary Nicholas, daughter of Thomas Lane, of Bentley, in the county of Stafford, a family as venerable for its antiquity as renowned for its loyalty, of which ye wonderful preservation of King Charles the Second, after the defeat of Worcester, is an instance never to be forgotten, in which glorious action she bore herself a considerable part, and that the memory of this extraordinary service might be continued to posterity, the family was dignified with a signal badge of honour—the Armes of England in a Canton.

Her sister Jane is better known, but Mary assisted her in no small way in effecting the escape of Charles. It is Mary who is the original of Sir Walter Scott's Alice Lee. I can never look at memorials in churches nor read their inscriptions nor the inscriptions on headstones in graveyards without wondering about the people so immortalized. Gallant Mary Lane of Staffordshire—how came she to meet a man from Manningford Bruce in Wiltshire? Manningford must have been a very small and isolated place in those days—it might still be called both—and then it was separated by much more than the miles from Staffordshire. Who was this Nicholas that travelled so far to woo? Hidden away in that tablet there is true romance. So much told us and so much more concealed. That crest, now: do Lanes or Nicholases still use it? On signet rings to seal letters, on silver spoons and forks at meal-times? Or has it all died, was posterity short-lived?

At Manningford the river, which had so far been flowing south-west, swings sharply to the south past the village of North Newton, where it is joined by yet another brook that has come through the heart of the Vale from Woodborough and beyond, and seems from the addition of these slight waters to gain yet greater strength. Though not yet an adult stream, it is now a stream on the very threshold of womanhood, bursting with life and eagerness, singing gaily in the little rapids, dancing over the stones, preening itself below the tall poplars. The hills rise again here, the long soft sweeps of the Downs on the southern edge of the Vale. Before me was the long line of Upavon Down rising to the aerodrome at the top, its sides dotted black-and-white with Friesian cattle. Here I was actually on the very skirts of Salisbury Plain. I was still in low country, a country of elms and ashes, and huge smooth, seemingly fenceless fields, but the ground was welling upwards. I came again to Scales

THE AVON AT
FIGHELDEAN,
FROM THE
MILL

WATTON'S FORD

Bridge, and now I could see away before me the crest of the Downs, the top, it seemed, of a high wall, a top crested against the evening sky with the humps of barrows.

It began to rain as I walked down the road into Upavon.

## CHAPTER II

## TO AMESBURY

I WAS recognized as soon as I opened the door of the public. In fact I received quite a flattering reception. Questions poured out. Had I found where the river began? Had I got myself wet finding it? " 'E's lost a mite o' stomach. Didun I tell 'ee, mister?" And so forth. (Actually, though they were all agreed that I had lost weight, they were all wrong. I put on weight when I am walking; I do not lose it. It is one of the minor trials of life for me. Not long ago I spent a summer walking for the B.B.C. and must have covered some four hundred miles or more altogether. I weighed fifteen stone when I started and rather more than sixteen stone when I finished. But people think that exercise necessarily entails a loss of weight, and so imagine that they see what they do not see. Even doctors seem to have this curious idea. When I asked my doctor how I could reduce my weight he suggested that I might take a brisk walk of a mile or so in the evening!) They were extremely interested in the course of the river—it was evident that there had been considerable discussion about it since my last visit—and very interested in the names of the two brooks that join at Upavon to form the river proper. Marden Brook they were prepared to accept, but Deane Brook or Deane Water they would have none of, despite the evidence of the Ordnance Map. "Never heard of it" was the general attitude, old and young alike. Pewsey Brook they were prepared to accept, but unwillingly; Deane was laughed to scorn. It would be interesting to know how the name Deane Water or Deane Brook arose.

Outside the rain was now coming down in earnest, driven on a light south-westerly breeze. Sleeping out, having left it so late, was not to be considered seriously, and fortunately

72

was not necessary. One of the best things about English villages is that there is always a barn or an out-house left unlocked, if you take the trouble to look carefully. And if you are careful to leave early, who is the wiser?

At Upavon the road divides. The main road runs on the left bank of the river, though actually some way from the stream itself, while a secondary road runs on the east bank and down in the valley itself. The main road, which is comparatively new, does not pass through any village (a few houses have sprung up along its length) and passes only an occasional lane. The secondary road, which follows much more closely the twists and turns of the river, runs through a succession of little villages and hamlets, and is obviously the old thoroughfare of the district.

It is at Upavon that the river, having gathered to itself the strength of the two brooks, throws itself at the great massif of Salisbury Plain, carving a long narrow cleft through its heart, down which it urges its bright waters. The road, for the early countryman was not one to neglect the aid of Nature, runs through this cleft, curving as the river curves in obedience to the commands of the chalk on either hand. A glance at the map showed clearly enough that I should not be able to follow the actual course of the river all the way down to Salisbury—too much of this land is in the hands of the military or the Air Ministry to allow of that—but by following the lower road and cutting across to the river whenever opportunity offered I should be keeping as close as conscience could want. And on the lower road I should pass villages and people, have the chance of conversation and entertainment, and I must admit that it was this, and not the demands of conscience that determined me to follow the lower road.

This is the valley down which Cobbett rode. This is the valley that roused him to such a fine wrath. I should like to quote in full here his entry for the ride from Milton to Salisbury, but it is a very long entry, such was his indignation, and I dare not do so in these days of short supply of paper. But you will remember that he gave a map with the entry showing the churches and manor houses lining the course of

73

the river from Wotton Rivers to Salisbury. He mapped in all
thirty-one churches and twenty-four manor houses in a distance
of some thirty miles—that does not allow for all the curves of
the river—and, even allowing for the fact that he made the
valley start at Wotton Rivers, where he thought that the river
rose, that still leaves thirty churches and the same number of
manor houses, since there was no manor house at Wotton
Rivers. Taking Cobbett as correct—and he was very careful
in matters of this sort—and omitting the churches at Fisherton
and Salisbury, for those would be in the town, that would
still leave seventeen churches between Upavon and Salisbury.
I am not concerned with the number of manor houses. I
am not quite sure what Cobbett really meant by a manor
house, and in any case economic conditions have changed so
much since his day that many a good manor may have become
a farm (as one, I know, has) and many may have been pulled
down, while some that I would not class as manors may
have been manors to Cobbett.

Cobbett was very struck with the number of churches in
so short a distance. He says :

It is manifest that the *population* of this valley was, at
one time, many times over what it is now ; for, in the
first place, what were the twenty-nine churches built *for* ?
The population of the twenty-nine parishes is now but
little more than one-half that of the single parish of Kensington ; and there are several of the churches bigger than
the church at Kensington. What, then, should all these
churches have been built *for* ? And besides, where did
the hands come from ? These twenty-nine churches
would now not only hold all the inhabitants, men, women,
and children, but all the household goods, and tools, and
implements, of the whole of them, farmers and all, if you
leave out the waggons and carts. In three instances,
Fifield, Milston, and Roach Fen, the *church-porches* will hold
all the inhabitants, even down to the bed-ridden and the
babies. What, then, will any man believe that these
churches were built for such little knots of people ? We

74

are told about the *great* superstition of our fathers, and of their readiness to gratify the priests by building altars and other religious edifices. But we must think those priests to have been devout creatures indeed if we believe that they chose to have the money laid out in *useless* churches, rather than have it put into their own pockets ! At any rate, we all know that Protestant priests have no whims of *this sort* ; and that they never lay out upon churches any money that they can, by any means, get hold of.

But suppose that we were to believe that the priests had, in old times, this unaccountable taste ; and suppose we were to believe that a knot of people, who might be crammed into a church-porch, were seized, and very frequently too, with the desire of having a big church to go to ; we must, after all this, believe that this knot of people were more than *giants*, or that they had surprising *riches*, else we cannot believe that they had *the means* of gratifying the strange wishes of their priests and their own not less strange *piety* and *devotion*. Even if we could believe that they thought that they were paving their way to heaven by building churches which were a hundred times too large for the population, still we cannot believe that the building could have been effected without bodily force ; and where was this force to come from, if the people were not more numerous than they now are ? What, again, I ask, were these twenty-nine churches stuck up not a mile from each other ; what were twenty-nine churches made *for*, if the population had been no greater than it is now ?

But, in fact, you plainly see all the traces of a great ancient population. The churches are almost all large, and built in the best manner. Many of them are very fine edifices ; very costly in the building ; and in the cases where the body of the church has been altered in the repairing of it, so as to make it smaller, the *tower*, which everywhere defies the hostility of time, shows you what the church must formerly have been. This is the case in several instances ; and there are two or three of these villages which must formerly have been *market-towns*, and particularly Pewsey and Upavon. There are now no less than nine of the parishes, out of the twenty-nine, that have either no parsonage-houses, or have such as are in such a state that a parson will not, or cannot, live in them. Three of them are poor, mean, falling-down places. This latter is the case at Upavon, which was formerly a very considerable place. Nothing can more clearly show, than this, that all, as far as buildings and population are concerned, has been long upon the decline and decay. Dilapidation after dilapidation have, at last, almost effaced even the parsonage-houses, and that too in *defiance of the law*, ecclesiastical as well as civil. The land remains ; and the crops and the sheep come as abundantly as ever ; but they are now sent almost wholly away, instead of remaining as formerly, to be, in great part, consumed in these twenty-nine parishes.

The *stars*, in my map, mark the spots where manor-houses, or gentlemen's mansions, formerly stood, and stood, too, only about sixty years ago. Every parish had its manor-house in the first place ; and then there were, down the valley, twenty-one others ; so that, in this distance of about thirty miles, there stood fifty mansion-houses. Where are they *now* ? I believe there are but eight that are at all worthy of the name of mansion-houses ; and even these are but poorly kept up, and, except in two or three instances, are of no benefit to the labouring people ; they employ but few persons ; and, in short, do not half supply the place of any eight of the old mansions. All these mansions, all these parsonages, aye, and their goods and furniture, together with the clocks, the brass kettles, the brewing-vessels, the good bedding and good clothes and good furniture, and the stock in pigs, or in money, of the inferior classes, in this series of once populous and gay villages and hamlets ; all these have been by the accursed system of taxing and funding and paper-money, by the well-known exactions of the state, and by the not less real, though less generally understood, extortions of the *monopolies* arising out of

76

paper-money; all these have been, by these accursed means, conveyed away, out of this valley, to the haunts of the tax-eaters and the monopolisers. There are many of the *mansion-houses* the ruins of which you yet behold. At Milton there are two mansion-houses, the walls and the roofs of which yet remain, but which are falling gradually to pieces, and the garden walls are crumbling down. At Enford Bennet, the member for the county had a large mansion-house, the stables of which are yet standing. In several places I saw, still remaining, indubitable traces of an ancient manor-house, namely a dovecote or pigeon-house. The poor pigeons have kept possession of their heritage, from generation to generation, and so have the rooks, in their several rookeries, while the paper-system has swept away, or rather swallowed up, the owners of the dove-cotes and of the lofty trees, about forty families of which owners have been ousted in this one valley, and have become dead-weight creatures, tax-gatherers, barrack-fellows, thief-takers, or, perhaps, paupers or thieves.

Cobbett made that entry on 30th August 1826. He was riding through a countryside grievously affected by the long Napoleonic Wars. He saw a countryside in the grip of Depression and Slump. On that scale, at least, it was a new phenomenon. But William Cobbett was not to know that what he was witnessing was to become the commonplace of rural lives, that in time it was even to affect urban lives. In his day post-war slump hit rural areas harder than it hit urban areas, for Britain was not yet industrialized. Cobbett was witnessing, though he did not know it, the end of an era. Never again was rural England to be truly prosperous.

Rather more than a century after Cobbett, in the same month, but in fact in another world rather than another century, I walked through the valley through which he had ridden. All the things which he saw on his travels through England, and which so infuriated him, have become part and parcel of our daily lives, so that we no longer really expect anything else, so that we do not really notice them any longer. Heavy Taxation—what did Cobbett know of that? Short Supply—we grumble, but do we really expect anything else now? Inflation—Cobbett saw inflation at work, though he did not know its name, what would he say if he knew what modern inflation was like and that no man would have the moral courage to acknowledge its existence? What Cobbett saw made him wrathful—and rightly so—but were he alive to-day to see what taxation is doing to the manor houses of Britain and to the landowners, could he, fiercely anti-clerical though he was, see the condition of the Church in Britain to-day, he would be appalled indeed: he would have apoplexy before he could write down one word of what he felt.

Yet, reading Cobbett, I wonder. Was this valley ever so populated as he believed it must once have been? Are big churches a sign of big population? Is even a ratio of a church to a mile, thick on the ground though that is, a sign of a big population? I am by no means convinced that it is. That the population of a valley such as this, the only truly fertile valley for miles on either hand, was once considerably bigger than it is now—bigger before Cobbett's day than when he made his journey—is almost certainly true. But it was never thickly populated. Had it been it would certainly have been visited by Celia Fiennes, for she was at Salisbury at the one end of the valley more than once and at Marlborough, near enough at the other end, on one occasion, and since she had a passionate interest in everything that was up-to-date and successful and prosperous she would have been certain to have heard of this populous, prosperous, church-laden valley. Defoe, too, would not have missed it, for he also had an incurable curiosity. Even had they both missed it, which I cannot believe, such a valley would have been bound to get into the news in some way or other, and so into the books, but there is no mention of it in any of the books in which you would expect to find it.

Churches, of course, have nothing whatever to do with population. Had the building of a church been contingent upon population none of our great cathedrals would have been built.  Salisbury in Celia Fiennes' day was but a small country town, yet she tells us that it had six churches, and she lived long before Cobbett, at a time when our population was even smaller.

The fact is that churches were built for two reasons. Firstly—I like to believe that this was indeed the first reason— because Man truly feared God, believed Him to be ever present and in full control of life in all its forms, and desired to do Him honour.  And, secondly, because the building of a church was a very concrete sign of the builders' prosperity and success in the world, something that the neighbours could not fail to see, and of which they would fully realize the importance.

That you can get some idea of the prosperity of a neighbourhood from its churches—that is the prosperity at the time of building—is true enough.  But the size of the church had nothing whatever to do with the size of the population, nor with the prosperity of all the people in the neighbourhood. It was a sign of the prosperity of the builder alone.  It was his income that regulated the building and its size, his income alone.  It must be remembered, too, that in those days the rich man had no fluid capital on which he could draw at a moment's notice.  His capital was in acres.  Possibly, he might borrow on those acres from some money-lender, but I think that this rarely happened.  Usually, I am sure, the amount of building completed in a year depended on what was saved from the estate during that year.  Both the progress of the building and its size must have depended on this. There is evidence enough that some of the big building schemes took years to complete, and were begun on very slender purses.  Chaucer, a man who missed nothing, a satirist perhaps, but an extremely observant man, gives us an insight into the methods by which a friary cloister was built. You will remember one of the brothers visiting a sick man to bring him comfort and consolation on his last bed?

> " Give me then thy gold, to make our cloister,"
> Quoth he, " for many a mussel and many an oyster,
> When other men have been full well at ease,
> Hath been our food, our cloister for to raise.

And yet, God wot, scarcely the fundament
Performed is, nor of our pavement
Is not a tile within our wones;
By God, we owe forty pounds for stones.
Now help, Thomas, for him that harrowed Hell.
For else must we our books sell.

So Chaucer in *Somnour's Tale*, and we may be sure that it was thus in many many cases. How much more difficult must have been the building of parish churches!

The big cathedrals and monastic churches were also big landowners, owning land sometimes in far distant parts of the country and building churches thereon, and they derived, in the later Middle Ages at any rate, a fair income from the gifts of pilgrims. (Though this could never have been a very safe source of income, since there appear to have been definite fashions in pilgrimage, the popularity of this or that saint rising and falling with the passing of the years.) But for the most part wealth came from land or cloth or shipping. Land in itself was not so valuable. There was little variation in crops throughout the crop-bearing soils, and crops were for the most part locally used. Sheep and wool were valuable, though. The great churches of the Cotswolds and Norfolk were built on the returns given by sheep, and those churches bore no relation whatsoever to the size of the population in those areas, only to the size of the pocket of the local magnate. This Avon Valley was never in the class of the Cotswolds or Norfolk as a sheep-rearing district, but this was sheep country and relatively prosperous and the churches, here as there, would be the local man's return for favours received. Whether the church was filled or not once it was built was a secondary consideration, if it was ever considered at all.

Yet, I think, Cobbett was right. I, too, think that Up-avon, which is now a village, and, despite the aerodrome and the traffic, rather a sleepy one, was once a small market town. It is, as I have said, a nice clean village with a pleasant smell of cows. But it still has about it an indefinable air of importance. Indeed, long long ago, away back in the time of Edward II, it was a market town, though then it would have had no greater population than it has now. Edward gave it to his favourite, Despenser, who, as have other favourites of monarchs, went mad. And then it was a cell of the Benedictine Abbey of Fontanelle in Normandy. There is no trace of all that now, of course, but there is still a very fine church, its Early English tower rising above the thatch of the village. The chancel is still, for the most part, transitional, and there is a quite remarkable chancel arch. Actually, there are three arches, the central one being Norman in part and wider than the others, of which the west one is rounded and the east one, which is narrower, pointed, while all the piers are square. This church was certainly built over a very considerable number of years, and perhaps the fine tower was the last thing in the main edifice to be constructed. That is, perhaps, late thirteenth century, while the chancel is middle twelfth, though the parapet is certainly fifteenth century. Here we have, I think, evidence for the lack of funds that must have been common to many builders. Again it is obvious that this church has been much reduced in size over the years. In this way, and in the rather slap-dash restoration that it has suffered from time to time it is disappointing, but the setting is magnificent and the view of the tower as you come into the village (from any direction) is most satisfying. Inside, I found it rather more than merely disappointing. The font, which is thirteenth-century work, eight-sided and with some lovely carving, is the only thing worth attention.

The deep cleft that begins at Upavon is guarded on either hand by ancient earthworks. On the west, high on the down, is Casterley Camp ; on the east, and almost exactly opposite, is Chisenbury Camp. Chisenbury is the smaller of the two and the outer rampart is lower. Casterley Camp covers some sixty acres, and I have heard it said, that this was the site of an ancient British township. Myself, though I am no archæologist, I doubt if any of these great earthworks were ever really townships, in the modern sense of that word. I suspect that it was the cattle and the sheep that went into the enclosed area, and that their owners slept and lived in the encircling ditches if they used them at all for that purpose. And yet, the position of these two earthworks, so obviously guarding the entrance to the valley (and the water route southwards) suggests that they were truly forts, even though at the time that they were built, man had a horror of the wooded low ground and kept so far as he was able to the open chalk tops. From the top of Chisenbury or Casterley you look down into a hollow, that gives the impression of being heavily wooded. The thatched gables of Upavon show through here and there, and the great tower of the church rises dominant above the trees. There is a gleam and sparkle from the little river, a true river now as it falls over a hatch into a deepening pool. It looked inviting, even in the drizzle that was steadily falling, and I went down to it.

It runs through a long very green meadow, and then again into the shelter of trees, twisting and turning by pollarded willows, through a withy bed (from which I disturbed a fox), then alder-fringed to more meadows, elm-studded, and so to the old manor house of Chisenbury. All the way, the Downs spread upwards to my left (they do so on the right also, though you are not so conscious of them), stretching away illimitable, their tops lost in the mist that was the drizzle I was experiencing. And for this I could be grateful, and was. For here and there, despite the draping drizzle, I could see the works of the military, black slugs carried on the fair breast of the down. It has never ceased to astonish me that, when a permanent encampment is being built by one of the Service Departments, so little attention is paid to appearance. This aerodrome has been here for many years now, and some care at least could have been expended on its architecture. It is the same everywhere. It would be difficult to imagine a more ugly, inconvenient and depressing place than Southampton Air-Port. The first impressions of thousands of visitors to Britain landing, as thousands do annually, at this ugly, rat-ridden collection of tin sheds must be harmful in the extreme to British prestige. You do not find anything like this at any foreign air-port—the one in Guernsey, for example, which is owned by the same Corporation, is a model of cleanliness and pleasant to look upon architecturally, too—but I know of no air-port in England that is not a jumble of ill-assorted tin. It seems evident that permanence means nothing to the Air Ministry, and that æsthetic values have never been considered. So, with the growth of man's business in the air, commercial and military, more and more of England's countryside is being disfigured to an extent that is quite unnecessary.

But the river was delightful and looked as though it would provide good fishing. There were fish moving, and I was for a moment tempted. A water vole splashed, forming rings on the surface as of a big fish rising, and moorhens spattered in and out of the withies. The steady drip of the heavens meant nothing to these water creatures. Indeed, there was perhaps a little more activity than there would have been on a fine warm day, for then, no doubt, there would have been men up and down the stream, danger abroad for the life of the water. But it was no day to linger and watch. I should be wet enough by eventide.

The hamlet of East Chisenbury lies on the river below the long slopes of Littlecot Down, whose crest carries the ramparts of a small earthwork now almost obliterated. The hamlet of West Chisenbury lies over the river on the main road, and beyond the Downs sweep up again to Widdington Farm below the eminence of Casterley. Here, in 1773, was born Henry Hunt, the friend of Cobbett, and, though less well-known (to-day not known at all), a very notable character. I imagine him to have been a typical Wiltshire farmer, farming on a large scale (chalk country farms are large to-day and have always been large), and strongly Tory in his views. That, indeed, would have been inevitable : farming on a large scale, on almost any scale, produces a firmly Tory outlook on life. The permanence of the soil, the ever-present sense of the past, the regular rhythm of the seasons, the slow tempo of the life can do no less. Farmers are not Tory by political conviction so much as by natural inheritance. So Hunt would have been a Tory, unaware, or but dimly aware, of any other political creed. He was a rich man, and widely noted as a sportsman and a breeder of fine horses. When the invasion scare came in 1801 he immediately offered his services and those of three mounted men, whom he would provide, clothe and pay. For some reason the offer was turned down by the commanding officer of the district, and Hunt was told that his services could be dispensed with. This, he regarded as an insult (which, indeed, it was) and as a reflection on his courage (which was probably not intended) and he challenged the soldier to a duel. For this he was fined one hundred pounds and given six weeks' imprisonment. He seems to have been confined in a cell with six other men of various degrees of social status, two of them habitual criminals. Brooding on his wrongs and meeting for the first time types entirely outside his world had a volcanic effect on him. He listened and learnt for the first time that life was not all that it had seemed to him, and he found for his own tale a most sympathetic audience. He went into prison a prosperous, but slighted, farmer. He came out a red-hot revolutionary. From thence on he became a national figure. He tried to get into Parliament for Bristol and failed ; he tried twice to persuade the electors of Somerset to return him, and failed ; eventually he entered Parliament as member for Preston. But he was not a success in the House and lost his seat after two years. But in the meanwhile he had acquired a tremendous reputation as an orator, and there were few men more feared by the landed classes (then in the fullest sense the rulers of the country) throughout Britain. Hunt was chairman and principal speaker at a gathering of more than 80,000 people at Manchester on the eve of the massacre of Peterloo. For his part there he was again arrested and again imprisoned—a longer sentence this—and this improved his position as a leader of the oppressed yet more. It is said that on his release he was met by the largest crowd that had ever gathered in London. By them he was carried shoulder-high through the streets to a rostrum from which he made yet another inflammatory speech, the while troops stood by not daring to interfere. Hunt had a glorious opportunity. But he went into Parliament, and that was the end of him as it has been the end of many another outstanding man. Pique has been the parent,

Parliament the pall, of many a revolutionary. I find comfort
in the thought in these days.

East Chisenbury has a small, but venerable and historic,
manor house. For many years it was the home of the Grove
family, but now with all the land hereabouts it belongs to the
State. It was in this small manor that Hugh Grove planned
with Colonel Penruddock the rising against Cromwell that
failed so tragically. More than two hundred gentlemen—
mainly from Wiltshire, Hampshire and Dorset—took part in
that adventure, riding in on the morning of March 11th 1655
to Salisbury and arresting the High Sheriff appointed by
Cromwell and his judges who were holding an assize. That
done they raised the Royal Standard and proclaimed Charles II
as King of England. For some days they held Salisbury, but
the citizens of that city did not move in their support, and
shortly the movement of Cromwell's troops forced them to
retreat south-westwards. At South Molton they were surrounded and captured, and Grove and Penruddock were
executed at Exeter. It was Penruddock who said on the
scaffold that he was to die for the crime of loyalty : it was
Grove who, standing at the foot of the scaffold awaiting his
turn to lose his head, shouted, " in this age called High
Treason ". The rising was in itself of small importance, but
it gave Cromwell the excuse, for which all dictators seek so
eagerly and find so easily, to put the whole country under the
control of the military.

Freed from the ancient mill-dam at Chisenbury the river
takes a big loop to the west, towards the main road, and flows
swiftly through open meadow-lands. The road climbs high
above it, so that you get a good view of the rich valley and
the river and the wild land sweeping up on either hand. It
is a bare bit of road this, with the outline of Celtic fields on
your left hand, their ridges pointing the bleakness, but fortunately the rain had stopped and brisk movement in the breeze
was drying me as I walked. Shortly the road dips to the
hamlet of Littlecot, which is itself one now with the hamlet
of Longstreet, and the two part of the village of Enford.
Here the river, split in characteristic chalk-stream fashion into

85

two or three channels, sweeps back to the road, and here was the ancient ford—Enford, of course, was Avon-ford—where the trackways, still visible and easy to be followed, came down off the hills. Enford church on the west bank is one of the more notable churches of the valley. I suppose that it might be called a Norman building, for the pillars and the arches are certainly of that period. The massive tower once carried a spire, but in 1817 that was struck by lightning and crashed on the main building, partially destroying it. The rebuilding was well done, but a further restoration in 1892 was not so fortunate. Even so, it is a dignified building.

Outside the inn at Longstreet stood a respectable gentleman in a dark suit, carrying an umbrella and a small black suitcase. He might well have been any city gentleman but for his face, which was the colour of old walnut, a complexion that can only be acquired through years of living in the open or an indiscretion on the part of one's mother. He greeted me as I approached :

" Good morning, good sir."

The voice was educated, the flowery speech accompanied by a gracious inclination of the head.

" Good morning," I said.

" Not the best weather for walking, though I have no doubt that you will have noticed that. Are you going far ? "

" Down the road."

" Salisbury way ? " I nodded. " Then I will accompany you a little, if you have no objection. Company makes the miles pass the more quickly."

He spoke carefully, each word meticulously pronounced, the speech of a Victorian schoolmaster, but it was not the careful speech of an uneducated man in fear of dropping his aitches. He swung into step beside me, and we set off down the road to Fittleton. He walked well with the long swing from the hips, slow-seeming, of the man accustomed to walking long distances. I noticed that his feet were shod in stout boots ; not the sort of footwear you expect with a dark, carefully pressed suit.

" You are on holiday, I presume, sir. A most healthy way

THE AVON AT AMESBURY

SALISBURY.  THE CATHEDRAL FROM ACROSS THE RIVER AVON

of taking a holiday too. Good for the body and good for the
soul. God's fresh air. But I see that you do not carry a
tent. Do you not find accommodation difficult to secure in
these small villages?"

He would not say "don't", but "do you not". A very
careful man in his speech. And perhaps a little curious.

"I am not on holiday," I said; "I'm working. And I
don't look for sleeping accommodation. I sleep out. It
saves trouble."

"Working?" His voice was sharp with curiosity.
"Might I presume so far as to enquire what work you do, my
good sir?"

"I write books," I said.

"Ah, and you are in search of copy, as I understand it is
called. Am I correct?"

"You are. And might I ask what you do? You're not
dressed for walking country lanes quite."

"I, too, am working, my good sir. I bring health and
comfort to these poor people. 'Health and cheerfulness
mutually beget each other'—if my memory serves me. And
in return for the service I do them, these kind people help me.
*Alterum alterius auxilio eget.* You will remember the line, of
course. Sallust, if my memory does not fail me, although it
is many years since I had traffic with the classics."

I had him placed now. "Oh, you're a crocus, are you?"

He stopped dead in his tracks, and looked at me. Then
he smiled, composure regained in the instant of its losing.

"I am somewhat astonished, my good sir, to find that you,
a man of education, a man of letters indeed, for have you not
told me that you write books, should be conversant with the
talk of the roads. But you are correct in your assumption.
I am a crocus, as you have, a little coarsely perhaps, termed it.
I prefer to think of myself as a doctor and of my profession
as that of medicine."

"You sound like a man of education yourself," I said.
"A man of letters for that matter. Anyway, you quote
Sallust at me, though it might have been Ovid for all I
know. . . ."

"Ovid!" He was genuinely shocked. "My dear sir, Ovid would never have written such a line."

"Maybe not. I don't know. Let's get back to the crocus. You carry the stuff in that little peter, I suppose? Doesn't look big enough for a day's work, not big enough to bring in a living anyhow."

"Peter! You must have spent some time on the road, my good sir, to have acquainted yourself so well with the rather specialized speech, if I may put it so. But again you are correct in your assumption. I do carry my medicines in this little suitcase. As to a living. Well, my good sir, what do you require of life? I require no more than good food and good drink and a good girl in my bed. Not *too* good, you understand." He gave a little high-pitched giggle and his mouth dropped. "Those are the essentials of life, my good sir, and you can get all of them in these villages. *All* of them." He giggled. "In every village." He giggled.

It began to rain again. "Christ Almighty, this —— rain." He stopped and opened his umbrella. He looked silly and out of place in his dark, carefully creased suit and neat Anthony Eden, carrying his little black suitcase, on that empty country road. Yet he had a certain dignity of appearance, so that my desire to laugh was stopped on my lips. But the essentials of life had ripped the care from his speech. The voice was still the voice of an educated man, but the mind had now forgotten all about the classics.

"Women," he said, "women pay for all this"—he waved the suitcase towards me—"but that's not what they want. Oh, dear me, no." He giggled. "Oh, dear me, no. What they want's the practised touch, different from these clods of husbands they've got. Women—fourteen I was——"

"I know," I said, "and it was your governess. And it's women made you a crocus. Go on."

If looks could have killed me. And then he grinned. The last hint of the careful pompous disappeared. "Wrong," he said. "You're quite wrong and you couldn't guess. Women? Yes, I suppose they are responsible in a way. Not that I'm grumbling. We must have been at Oxford about the same time, I should think. Well, you know how it was. All right if you'd a strong will or no money or no spunk. All right if you were going to get a blue or a first or something. But I'd no character and not enough money. I suppose I might have got a good degree—they told me so anyhow—but I liked the girls too much and the wine. You know how it is." He giggled.

"Well, what did you do, when you got sent down?" I asked.

"Entered the scholastic profession." He declaimed the words. "Prep. school. Headmaster's wife. Caught *in flagrante delicto*. Marvellous. I can see his face now. Marvellous. But the old boy gave me a jolly good testimonial. A maid at the next place, and, well, you know how it is. So, now, I'm a crocus—and a bloody good life too."

"But where do you get your scoff in these places?"

There was no question now at my using "specialized speech". He had accepted me as a man of the road, together with all that it implied.

"Oh, I never have to go into the dining-rooms—except when I'm in Salisbury or Devizes; they're the limits of my beat. I can get a meal in any of these villages. You see, the men are usually out, all day, and the poor wives lonely. Oh yes, I can get a meal all right. Never go to a lettary either, except in the towns. Know what a lettary is, don't you?"

"Oh yes. I've been in them." (Lettaries, for the uninitiated, are lodgings which let bed and breakfast for 3s. 6d. or 1s. 9d. if you share the bed with another man. I have not yet shared a bed.)

"And scarpered, too, I'll bet." (Scarper means to go off without paying the bill.) "No letties for me, thank *you*. They like me coming round. Welcome. The practised touch, you see." He giggled. "By God, I could tell you a thing or two."

"I'm sure you could," I said. And he proceeded to do so. Out of that educated mouth in cultured accents poured the most astonishing stream of pornographic reminiscence I have ever had the good fortune to listen to. How much of it was true, I could not possibly say, but I fancy that a good deal of it was. And how he loved it. His mouth loose, the saltiest bits punctuated with a girlish giggle, he revelled in reminiscence. And so we came to Fittleton with myself a good deal wiser about men and women than when the day had started. The rain had stopped again as we came to the outskirts of the village. Down came the umbrella, and he carefully smoothed himself down. Suddenly he said, " That was good copy, you know, and every bloody word true. What's it worth ? " He stood facing me in the road, and he looked nasty. I did not feel very happy, having a horror of rows of any sort.

" Nothing," I said.

" Why, you bloody . . ."—the words tumbled out, a great spate of blasphemy and obscenity. He poked his umbrella at me. It fell short by an inch or two, and he shuffled a bit nearer. " You ——." He dribbled at the mouth. " You ——. You ——. I'll have the —— off you." The words came out with educated nicety of precision. And all the time he shuffled forward, and all the time I edged backward. Smaller than myself by a good deal, shorter and lighter, he still did not look a pleasant customer and I was scared stiff of what was about to happen. I slung the rucksack off my back—you cannot fight with a rucksack hampering you—and as I did so, while it was still half on, he was close, his umbrella jabbing at me purposefully. Then suddenly he stopped, standing still in the road, leaning on his umbrella. A car came round the bend. I had not heard it, but he, accustomed no doubt to keeping one ear open, had. The car swept up, the driver throwing a curious glance at us as he passed. But the brief interval was enough. My rucksack was on the ground, and there was a yard between us. He looked at me coldly, but the savagery had gone from his eyes. He leaned a little on his umbrella, then smiled—a charming smile, too—raised his hat with all the courtesy that a good public school can teach its members, and said :

" Good day to you, my dear sir. I have greatly enjoyed our walk and our conversation. *Sed deficit omne quod nascitur.*

There is a church in the village here, which, I understand, is worthy of attention. Good day to you, my dear sir."

He put on his hat, swung on his heel and walked sedately down the road, neatly dressed, black suitcase in one hand, umbrella swinging with just the right degree of jauntiness in the other, the very model of respectability. I sat on the roadside and watched him go. I have never been more thankful to see the back of a man. Rarely have I experienced a more uncomfortable minute or so. A rather frightening little man. I sat on the roadside and thanked heaven for that car and smoked a pipe. It would do no harm, I thought, to let him get into the village and about his business or his women. I did not want another meeting.

But there is only the one road through Fittleton, which is a hamlet rather than a village even though it is now to all intents and purposes joined on to Haxton, and there he was, standing at a cottage door, his suitcase open on the step, himself engaged in conversation with the housewife, a nice respectable-looking body. He saw me, of course, and raised his hat, calling out : " Do not forget to see the church, my dear sir." As polite as could be, then turning again to business, all courtesy to the lady. An eminently respectable salesman.

I took his advice and went into the church. It is a pleasant building, small and I should guess of late thirteenth-century construction, with a western tower that must be a good deal more recent, perhaps late fifteenth. In the chancel arch there are two squints, now stopped, and the font is definitely Norman. In the chancel there is a fine altar tomb to one of the Hicks Beach family, and I remembered that I was nearing Netheravon where that family showed Cobbett such grand sport. Yes, a charming little church, not in any way notable, but more full of atmosphere than one expects nowadays to find in small village churches. I came out again into the village and walked on towards Haxton, keeping a sharp eye for the crocus, whose company I did not want on the road to Netheravon. But there was no sign of him.

Netheravon has grown a good deal of recent years, and

not for the better. But the river has not altered at all. It has not yet the appearance of a big stream, but it is, here, taking on the quality of manhood. Here and there are little rapids, where the water swirls angrily over stones or round obstructions ; here and there the banks are eaten away by a force stronger than themselves. Looking down on the stream from one of the little heights around, and noticing the deep purposeful curves, you realize suddenly, as you have not so far noticed in all its course, a relentless power.

This is fishing water. And I saw scarcely a fish. I should imagine that it must rank among the most consistently flogged water in all Britain, and flogged by many unskilful anglers at that. It looked tempting enough, but there was nothing to tempt, and I explored this reach thoroughly, feeling the likely lies and watching the run of the current. There are fish, of course—no doubt plenty of them—but they have learned wisdom and stay down. I had a feeling that it would be a master fly-fisherman who could fill a creel legitimately on this water.

There is still much that is beautiful about Netheravon, especially the church, which is one of the finest village churches in all Wiltshire. It has a very fine Norman doorway in the tower, and there are Norman arches in the belfry and the chancel. I like, too, the lancet windows with their very wide splays in the clerestory. But it is the tower that is of particular interest, because you cannot quite make up your mind, looking at it, whether it is Saxon work or early Norman. The local inhabitants, I believe, prefer to call it Saxon, which is understandable, but I personally think that it is a very fine example of very early Norman building. The parson here for two years, 1794 to 1796, was Sydney Smith, who had some reputation as a wit. On the whole he seems to have had a pretty thin time of it while in charge of Netheravon, for Lady Holland tells us that " he often dined on a mess of potatoes sprinkled with a little ketchup ". In those days the butcher's cart came over from Salisbury only once a week, but in any case Smith had so little money that he could not have bought sufficient meat to provide him with more than a couple of meat meals in the week. But he did have a very good friend in the squire, Hicks Beach, and it was the squire who shortly launched him and his rather extensive repertoire of bad jokes on the world.

It was this Hicks Beach who was the friend of Cobbett.

Not far above Amesbury is a little village called Nether-haven, where once I saw an *acre of hares*. We were coursing at Everly, a few miles off; and one of the party happening to say that he had seen " an acre of hares " at Mr. Hicks Beech's at Netherhaven, we, who wanted to see the same, or to detect our informant, sent a messenger to beg a day's coursing, which being granted, we went over the next day. Mr. Beech received us very politely. He took us into a wheat stubble close by his paddock; his son took a gallop round, cracking his whip at the same time; the hares (which were very thickly in sight before) started all over the field, ran into a *flock* like sheep; and we all agreed that the flock did cover *an acre of ground*. Mr. Beech had an old greyhound, that I saw lying down in the shrubbery close by the house, while several hares were sitting and skipping about, with just as much con-fidence as cats sit by a dog in a kitchen or a parlour. Was this *instinct* in either dog or hares? Then, mind, this same greyhound went amongst the rest to course with us out upon the distant hills and lands; and then he ran as eagerly as the rest, and killed the hares with as little remorse. Philosophers will take a long while before they will make men believe that this was *instinct alone*. I believe that this dog had much more reason than half the Cossacks have; and I am sure that he had a great deal more than many a negro that I have seen.

Natural history was not Cobbett's strong point. But the hares are still around Netheravon. Not in such numbers, it is true—you would never now see an acre of them—but there are still more hares to be seen around here than, I believe, anywhere else in the south of England. Almost every time I cast my eye over a field or scanned the face of a down, there

was a hare, perhaps several, to be seen. And hares are extremely easy to catch ! Living in this valley cannot be bad, even in these days of rationing.

The Hicks Beach house now belongs to the Crown, like almost everything else in this neighbourhood. It is no good pretending that the military have not made a difference to the district. They have for one thing brought in a good deal of money—the local inns benefit considerably—and for another they have put up a lot of building that is hideous in the extreme. But, even so, they have not to any great extent affected the landscape. These downs, these water-meadows, these lanes—even in essence these villages—are very much the same now as they were a hundred years ago. There is plenty of red brick, garish and foreign, plenty of corrugated iron (the countryman's stand-by for all emergencies), but there are still plenty of tall elms, plenty of flint and chalk. " Progress " has made inroads, but it has not yet conquered entirely. And there is still the vastness of the Plain beneath a sky that appears as wide as all the Universe. True, as you look, the eye is caught—too often caught—by some ghastly military monstrosity, there are blots and scars all over the horizon, but there is still more space untouched than touched. It is inevitable, of course, that this scarring should have happened to the Plain. The place is an ideal training ground for soldiers —even in these days of atoms and mechanization, it is ideal— and soldiers must be trained. There is always much talk about the bare expanses of moorland in the west, in Wales, in Scotland (and much of that, too, has fallen prey to the military), but none can compare with this rolling plateau for the purpose. And I must confess that, if something has got to go, as it has, I would rather see Salisbury Plain altogether ruined from the tourist point of view than the wild moorlands of the west and north. In any case it will not be altogether ruined ; it is too vast for that, even in these wholesale-slaughter days. And the Avon, at least, has not been affected. It still glides peacefully between willow-screened water-meadows, from mill to mill, and the meadows are still as generous to the farmer as in olden days. The plover still come down in the winter, the larks still rise throughout the year. The farmers still grumble and still retire (if a farmer ever does) rich men. Cobbett would not recognize much that is here now, but there is yet much that is just the same now as when he rode down this valley all those years ago.

The inn at Netheravon is not in the village proper, but on the main road on the west side of the valley above the river. It is the first inn on this main road since Upavon, and it does a very brisk trade during the few hours that modern Government will allow. I walked up to it, and spent a little time sitting and talking to labourers and to a brick-faced sergeant of engineers, and then walked on down the main road, so that I might look across to the sweeping downs eastwards and down on the river winding in deep curves through the steep valley.

I had intended to cross again by the ford to Figheldean and walk the east side of the valley to Milston a couple of miles further on, but very shortly after leaving Netheravon I was overtaken by a young woman on a bicycle. It was one of those bicycles with handlebars sweeping downwards towards the hub of the front wheel, so that the rider has his or her head below the level of the backside as often as not. They are, no doubt, excellent machines for swift travel (personally I find bicycling the most tiring form of progression imaginable, and find myself walking and pushing much more frequently than riding) but they do not—there can be no question whatever about this—suit the female figure. They would not suit the female figure in skirts, but these bicycling women wear shorts, and so succeed in making themselves yet more grotesque. It was not, therefore, with any pleasure that I saw this girl dismount and wait for me to overtake her. She was short and well-built enough to be called stout. Beneath a mop of bobbed fair hair, she had a pleasant open face, and beneath the waist, ill-concealed by a very short pair of khaki shorts, she had a pair of fat dimpled knees. The shorts were stretched as tight as the skin of a pre-war sausage.

She grinned as I came up. " Hallo ; you come far ? "

Miles and miles, I assured her. "And you?"

"From London," she said. "Been in Marlborough, seeing my sister. She's in service, there. I'm going to Exeter; where you going?"

"Christchurch," I said.

"Coo, where's that? Is it a nice place?"

"No," I said firmly. "It's a horrible place. I wouldn't dream of going there, if I hadn't got to."

"Oh! Where you sleeping to-night?"

"I've no idea," I said. "Somewhere around here, I expect. Anywhere."

She, it appeared, had bed-and-breakfasted it all the way from London, and would find somewhere in Salisbury that night. She wanted to see the cathedral, which surprised me. Oh, she liked cathedrals; you could sit and eat your sandwiches in them and it was nice and quiet, and no one bothered you. She liked cathedrals, though she was a Baptist, mind you, at least her people were. She chattered away, ninety to the dozen, pushing her bicycle and keeping pace with me. She was surprised that I slept out with no tent or anything. She wouldn't like that, she thought. I wouldn't like bed-and-breakfast places night after night, I told her. Oh, they weren't bad on the whole. Good food as a rule, better than what you got in hotels and inns, and the beds were clean. It was the men that were the trouble, couldn't leave a girl on her own alone. But she did not look as if that troubled her a lot. This was her holiday, she said, and she had started out with her young man from London, but they had quarrelled very soon. "Trying to jump the fences," she said enigmatically. And while I was wondering which was the fence he had fallen at, she said, somewhat surprisingly: "I know who you are. I've been wondering all the while where I'd met you before, but, of course, I haven't. It's your voice. You broadcast, don't you? Sundays mainly. I always listen. And you were doing some walks a year or so back, when I was on holiday in Devonshire, and my sister and I went out to see if we could meet you. Brian Vesey-FitzGerald, isn't it?"

"Yes," I said. "It is. I didn't know my voice was all that uncommon, though."

"Coo. Fancy meeting you like this. Peg will be furious when I get to Exeter. Peg's another sister; she works in Exeter. Coo." And then, to my intense astonishment, she began to talk most knowledgeably about birds. She really did know a lot about them, and she was obviously frantically keen about them. "I always get the bird books from the library," she said. And when I said that it was a strange taste for a young woman working in London, she said that it was her father. He'd been a porter at some small station in the country in Sussex, and the son of a gamekeeper, and now he was in London, but still at heart in Sussex and all three daughters had his tastes. "I go out to the reservoirs at Staines most Sundays," she said. "Wonderful what you see there. I love it. Other Sundays we go out to Purley or somewhere. Quite good that is, too, in its way."

Listening to her chatter, I passed Figheldean without noticing the turning. But above Milston, looking across the valley, I could see the corrugated town of Bulford, and away beyond the distant heights around Tidworth. There was a faint rumble in the air from gun-fire. Assheton Smith hustled his foxes about up there. I wonder what he would have thought of it all now. Cobbett would not, I fancy, have been shocked, for Cobbett was a severely practical man; but Assheton Smith would have bemoaned the fate of the English countryside in this twentieth century. The tin nightmare that is Bulford recalled me to a sense of duty.

"I've got to go down here," I said, pointing to Milston.

"Oh, what's there?"

"Nothing at all," I said. "Absolutely nothing. Just a small village, and a church, not a very beautiful church or anything. That's all."

"Then why go?" she asked, reasonably enough. "Want to get rid of me?"

"Oh no," I said. "I'm supposed to be walking this river here. It's a job of work. And I ought to be down there by it."

I could not have said anything more likely to arouse her curiosity, I realized too late.

" A job of work ?  Ooh, you are going to broadcast on this walk, like you did the others.  Goodee, I'm coming too. I've never seen a broadcast."

" But I'm not going to do a broadcast, I promise you. Really I'm not.  I'm walking this river because I'm going to write a book about it.  That's all, and I really must see the villages along the way.  I've missed one already talking to you, and I cannot miss two."

The book was almost as bad.  She wanted to know all about it, when it was coming out and all that.  I said—perfectly truthfully, for even publishers do not seem to know when their books are coming out nowadays—that I had not the slightest idea, and anyway I had not yet written a word.

" But you will put me in it, won't you ?  After all, I have walked a bit of the way with you."

She looked quite anxious about it.  " Oh yes," I said ; " I'll put you in it.  Promise."  She pressed a bit more, but in the end she seemed satisfied, though she insisted on giving me her address so that I could let her know when the book was published and she could get it out of the library.  Then she mounted her bicycle, and disappeared at an astonishing pace down the road to Amesbury.  She was a nice girl.

Milston is a pretty little place, half-enclosed by the river. Down in the valley the corrugated mass of Bulford is hidden, and, except for the steady rumble of gun-fire, this might have been the world of William Cobbett.  But there is nothing in the least noteworthy about Milston, except that it has managed to maintain its identity all these years solely on the labours of a few farmers.  The church is small and undistinguished and there is not even an inn.  But it was here that Joseph Addison was born, the son of the parson of the place, and though he did not write his poem, which is now a hymn, here I think that there can be no doubt at all that the author of the *Highways and Byways* volume was right, and that it was the sight of the Downs rising so steeply all around, the great Salisbury Plain sky, that inspired it :

The spacious firmament on high,
With all the blue ethereal sky,
And spangled heavens, a shining frame,
Their great Original proclaim.

Th' unwearied Sun, from day to day
Does his Creator's power display;
And publishes to every land
The works of an Almighty hand.

Soon as the evening shades prevail.
The Moon takes up the wondrous tale;
And nightly to the listening Earth
Repeats the story of her birth:

Whilst all the stars that round her burn,
And all the planets in their turn,
Confirm the tidings as they roll,
And spread the truth from pole to pole.

Not a great poet, Addison. And perhaps, that was the only poetry that he ever wrote. Better as a hymn than a poem it undoubtedly is, but if you stand in Milston and look upwards you cannot fail to see what Addison saw, and understand how he felt. There is just that infinitude.

It is but another three miles down the river to Amesbury, and it was there that I intended to sleep. But to go on down the east bank of the stream meant passing hard by Bulford, and that was more than I could bear. So I crossed the river again and made my way to Durrington. In fact you do more than cross the river here, you cross rivers. The Avon is now beginning to take on the one great characteristic of chalk streams, and to divide and divide again into many little streams. Here it is still easy to tell the main stream from its children, but here, as is so often the case with chalk streams, the minor waters are more attractive than the parent stream.

Durrington itself is nothing to look at. You would pass through it without a second thought, and, so far as architecture goes, small blame to anyone who does. But Durrington is a place of great antiquity. Close by the modern village at Durrington Walls there was a British village, and there are old green roads hereabouts that are to this day as they were, say, two thousand years ago—the Wiltway and the Packway, and others that are nameless. The Packway runs off the main road on to the Plain, the main road itself runs through the earthwork of Durrington Walls, cutting the area enclosed by the embankment roughly in half.

It is a curious earthwork, this at Durrington. Like that at Avebury the ditch is on the inner side of the bank, so the place could not have been used for defence. The whole area enclosed is some thirty acres, and more or less circular in shape. On the western side, adjoining the ditch there is a small rectangular enclosure, which may not be of the same date as the rest of the earthwork. Cultivation has damaged the whole a great deal; the earthworks are much lowered, and it is difficult now to get a clear picture of what was once here. On the whole it seems likely that the place was used for some ceremonial purpose.

West of Durrington lies Lark Hill Camp, and the whole area around has been much defaced by military buildings, so that one is disinclined to explore. A look, one would think, was sufficient. But the whole area contains besides the military a wealth of prehistoric monument. Woodhenge, for example, lies within the parish boundary of Durrington.

Woodhenge was discovered by Squadron-Leader Insall, V.C., on December 12th, 1925. He was then flying at 2,000 feet over Stonehenge, and noticed a circle with white chalk marks in the centre near Durrington Walls. It looked very similar to Stonehenge, which he could, of course, see at the same time. Later he photographed it, and there were white chalk marks in the plough. Later still, flying as the sun was setting, he noticed that there was a distinct depression inside the outer circle and a gradual mound in the centre, both clearly revealed by the shadows cast by the low sun. He made enquiry and was told that it was only a mutilated disc-barrow, but this did not satisfy him and he waited to see what would be revealed when the crops were up. Then there was no further doubt at all. He photographed it again, and there were five or six, perhaps even seven, closely set rings. Woodhenge was discovered.

Excavation on the site was begun in August 1926. There were found six concentric circles, oval rings of holes that had once held timber posts, the holes of the different rings being of different sizes. Near the centre, relatively in the same position as the Altar Stone at Stonehenge, there was found the burial place of a young child, whose skull had been cleft before burial, which suggests a dedicatory rite, but not necessarily human sacrifice. Below the floor of the ditch in the eastern sector was found the crouched skeleton of an adult.

Woodhenge, in fact, bears many similarities to Stonehenge. It is much simpler and much ruder in design, but it is difficult not to believe that the same overwhelming feeling dictated the building of both monuments. Both were surely ceremonial places, the one in stone and the other in wood. It has been suggested that Woodhenge was the forerunner of Stonehenge, that the builders tried out their prentice hands here before starting work on the greater building. I am no archæologist, but I must confess that I find that difficult to believe. All the knowledge that went to the building of the even greater temple at Avebury cannot have been lost. Avebury must still have been standing, if not whole, as nearly whole as would make no difference. The builders would have but to go and look. No, I feel sure that Woodhenge played some particular part in the ceremonies of this ancient civilization. To look at it now, with its little rows of white posts showing the sites of the original timber posts, it is decidedly unimpressive. I, at least, find myself quite unable to get any impression of what the original monument must have looked like : I can get no impression of its size, but little of its shape. Possibly that is revealed only to the trained eye of the professional archæologist. I have a feeling that the only way the amateur could ever grasp the whole would be from an aeroplane as was the good fortune of Insall.

I turned away rather depressed by this wonder of our ancient world, and walked the short quarter of a mile to the Cuckoo Stone. This is a single sarsen stone. It has been suggested that it was used to mark the equinox as observed from Woodhenge, but that does not impress me at all. It is easy to make the fact of its presence fit this or that theory, but the theories remain theories. The stone might have fitted any one of a number of other purposes ; it might have fitted no purpose at all. It might, in fact, have been discarded on its way to Stonehenge (builders have been known to leave bricks about before now), it might have been surplus to requirements (though I doubt if the ancient Office of Works used such ridiculous language as the modern), it might just have been dropped. The fact is that it is there. It is the sort of thing that one would expect legend to have gathered around. I do not know of any legend, and I could hear of none on enquiry in Amesbury. But it is not difficult to see what sort of legend—and not legend to begin with—was attached to it. In a terrier of the parish of Durrington, dated late in the eighteenth century, it is referred to as the " Cuckoldston " and in a deed, dated 1819, the land is called " Cuckoldston Acre". Some frolicsome wife was caught here at some time, though it must have made a hard bed indeed.

While I was looking at the stone it began to rain again, and before I had reached the main road it was coming down in steady earnest, so thickly that the Downs on the other side of the valley were shut from view. It was evident that this time it was not going to stop, this was the beginning of a wet night. No sense in lingering on the road now, no sense in going down to the river to see the junction of Nine Mile River (which is really but a little stream) with the main water, as I had intended to do. The obvious thing to do was to get into Amesbury as quickly as possible.

A soaking wet evening is not the best time to see Amesbury. The place seemed deserted, dead and dripping. Yet even so there was a dignity about it that was impressive. That is proper : for Amesbury is the chief and oldest place in all the valley of the upper Avon.

The very name is pregnant with history and legend. Amesbury is but a modern corruption of Ambrosebury, Ambrose's Town. It is said—and I cannot see any reason at

THE TOWN BRIDGE OVER THE AVON AT SALISBURY

WILTON. THE
RIVER WYLYE

all why it should not be true—that it was here that Ambrosius Aurelianus was born, that it is here he lies buried. There are still those who maintain that Ambrosius is a legendary figure, as they maintain Arthur to be, and it is true enough that there is little in the Dark Ages that followed the withdrawal of the Romans which can with any certainty be sifted from the mass of legend. Arthur has become part of our folk-lore, and that makes it all a little more difficult. His deeds have been chronicled in song and ballad, in story and poetry, and there is wrapped round him now a cloak of myth through which it is almost impossible to see. But that is no sound reason for denying that he ever lived. So far as Ambrose is concerned we have the support of history. That support is lacking for Arthur, but for myself I have no doubt whatever that he did live.

It is true that we know nothing at all of his real life. We do not know where he was born. It is a tradition in Cornwall that he was a Cornishman and that Tintagel was his birthplace: Hampshire would have it that he was a Winchester man: Wales that he was a Welshman. It seems probable that he had his beginnings somewhere in the West, and for myself I admit to believing Wales more probable than Cornwall. As to what he was : we have no knowledge whatever of his rank or parentage. There is no evidence that he was a king, and he was most certainly not King of all Britain. (Nennius says that he fought with the king of the Britons and was their leader in war, but he does not say at any time that he was himself a king.) It may be that he was the son of a British chief (but surely if that was the case Nennius would have described him as of royal blood ?), more likely, perhaps, that he was a member of some great Roman family that remained behind after the withdrawal of the legions. Be that as it may he must have belonged to a family distinguished enough to give him the right to speak in the presence of the country's great men. But we know nothing for certain. He appears suddenly in the darkest period of our history, a more than life-size figure, a great military leader. We are told that he was the general in command of the

British forces at the time when the Saxons were threatening
the land and the remnants of the old Romano-British civilization was struggling desperately to keep its head above the
turbulent waters of successive pagan waves. We are told
that he won for his country after twelve great battles (all of
them in places that cannot now be identified with certainty)
a much-needed period of peace. The greatest of these
victories was that of Mount Badon, and after it there was
twenty-one years of peace, and then his great work was
destroyed not by pagan invasion but by dissension among
the Britons themselves. Arthur himself fell at the battle of
Camlann (and where was that?) and presumably he was
buried, but no one knows where. Tradition—but a very
much later tradition—insists that he did not die, but that he
was magically transported to Avalon (and where is that?)
and that one day, when his country needs him most, he will
return. That is a legend that is common to folk-heroes all
over the world. We have it also with Drake and his drum.

It is a curious thing that only two early historians mention
him by name. They are Nennius, who wrote early in the
ninth century, and the compiler of the *Annales Cambriæ*,
whose story ends with the year 977. There is an earlier
historian—Gildas. Gildas was born in the year of the victory
of Mount Badon. His boyhood would, therefore, have
coincided with the last years of the life of Arthur. Yet
Gildas makes no mention at all of Arthur. He refers to the
battle of Mount Badon, but he does not name the general
who won it. Throughout his impassioned account of the
troubles of the Britons, throughout his violent attack on the
sins of his countrymen, he makes no mention whatever of
Arthur. He speaks only of Ambrosius Aurelianus, who was
Arthur's immediate predecessor as leader of the Britons.
Reading Gildas you would have no knowledge of Arthur:
so far as Gildas is concerned it would seem that Arthur did
not exist. The Venerable Bede, who relied on Gildas for
this early period in our history, naturally makes no reference
to Arthur. The *Anglo-Saxon Chronicle* ignores him and
Ambrosius. And yet the tradition has grown.

Ambrosius is a different matter. The withdrawal of the Roman garrison in the early part of the fifth century left Romanized (and largely Christian) Britain exposed to the attacks of the Scots in the north and the Saxons all along the east and south coasts. They were nasty raids but they did not interrupt the whole life and economy of the country. Constantius writing of the visit of St. Germanus in 429 says that he found the people Christian and civilized, well able to defend themselves against raiders, following a well-ordered way of life. Indeed, he speaks of Britain as " that most wealthy island ". It was not, in fact, until the middle of the century that Saxon invasion began in earnest, to be followed by settlement on conquered land. The chroniclers all blame King Vortigern for allowing the Saxons to gain a foothold. Vortigern in the face of invasion by the Picts and subjected to attack by Ambrosius (we are not told why there was this internal strife, but it is evident that Ambrosius was the leader of the West) called in Saxon mercenaries. They established themselves firmly in Kent, and later, as is the way of mercenaries the world over, turned on their employers. Gildas describes how Vortigern called a Council meeting and how :

all the councillors, together with their haughty king, were so blinded that (devising a help, say rather a destruction for the country) they introduced those ferocious Saxons of unspeakable name, hateful to God and men, bringing as it were wolves into the fold in order to beat back the nations of the North.

And he goes on to tell how these mercenaries, reinforced from abroad, picked quarrels over the question of supplies, and how " a fire of just vengeance by reason of our former sins " spread over the country. He describes the devastation of the countryside and the sacking of the towns :

Terrible it was to see, in the midst of the streets, tops of towers torn from their lofty fittings, the stones of the high walls, holy altars, fragments of bodies, covered with clotted blood, so that they seemed as if squeezed together in some ghastly wine-press. There was no burial for the dead, save in the ruins of their homes, or the bellies of beasts and birds (with all reverence to the blessed souls, if indeed many such were found, which at that time were carried by the holy angels to Heaven) . . . some of the wretched remnant were caught in the mountains and all murdered there ; others, forced by famine, surrendered, to be forever the slaves of their foes, if indeed they were not slain on the spot, verily the greatest favour ; others with great wailing sought the regions beyond the sea. . . .

But some hid to form in due course the army of Ambrosius, that " Modest man, who alone of the Roman nation was left alive amid the tumult of so troubled a time ". Gildas is enthusiastic about Ambrosius. He speaks of him as " courteous, faithful, valiant, and true, a man of Roman birth who had alone survived the conflict, his kindred who had worn the purple having perished in the struggle ; his descendants, greatly degenerated in these days from the excellence of their ancestors, still provoke their conquerors to battle, and, by the Grace of God, their prayers for victory are heard ". Under this model of manhood the tide of disaster was turned. From the appearance of Ambrosius on the scene things were more or less equal—sometimes the Britons were successful and sometimes the Saxons, with a bias in favour of the Britons—until the battle of Mount Badon, a battle which Gildas describes as " almost the last slaughter of these gallows-birds, but by no means the least ". But he does not tell us the name of the general who contrived this great victory.

It is possible that Gildas thought that anything that had happened so recently was too well-known to need recording. He could not have known that he was writing for posterity. He was at pains to bring history up-to-date, no more than that. He wished to bring the dim past to the knowledge of his countrymen, the recent past and the present was known well enough. The fact that Gildas did not mention Arthur does not mean that there was no such person. Nennius, however, does state definitely that Arthur was the victor of

Mount Badon. In his *Historia Brittonum* he refers to Arthur without explanation or introduction. He could only have done so if he was certain that all his readers would be thoroughly familiar with his name. Nennius says of the war between the Britons and the Saxons :

> When Hengest was dead, Octha his son crossed from the north part of Britain to the kingdom of Kent. From him the kings of Kent spring. Then Arthur fought against them in those days, with the kings of the Britons, but he was their leader in war. The first battle was at the mouth of the river Glein. The second, and the third, and the fourth, and the fifth on another river called Dubglass, in the land of Linnius. The sixth, on the river called Bassas. The seventh in the wood Celidon, that is *Cat Coit Celidon* (the battle of the wood Celidon). The eighth was the battle in Castle Guinnion, in which Arthur carried on his shoulders the representation of the Blessed Virgin Mary, and the heathen were turned to flight in that day, and great was the slaughter of them, through the virtue of our Lord Jesus Christ and His mother, the Blessed Virgin Mary. The ninth battle was in the City of the Legion. He fought his tenth battle on the shore of the river called Tribuit. The eleventh battle was in the mountain called Agned. The twelfth battle was on Mount Badon, in which there fell in one day 960 men from the onslaught of Arthur only, and no one laid them low, save he alone. And in all his battles he was the victor.

Already Arthur is the Christian leader defending his country against pagan invaders ; already he has stature ; already he is a hero ; already so well known that he needs no introduction. Already there are legends gathered round his name.

Quite fantastic stories have gathered around Arthur, and for so long now that they hide completely his historicity. It is easy to dismiss him as a shadow god, the imaginary creation of a backward and illiterate people. But, in fact, it is these very legends, these very fantastic tales, that substantiate his historicity. So far from being proof that their central figure is mythical, they are surely proof that he existed in flesh and blood. They are just the sort of tales that one would expect to gather round the name of a great leader, victorious in troubled and dangerous times, after his death. They are just the sort of tales that a conquered and enslaved people would tell to support them in misery. The man himself would be forgotten, but what he stood for and the glory that was then is never forgotten. The greater the misery, the greater the legend : it is so in every country.

The legends grew with the passing of the years, soon grew beyond the bounds of history and entered the wonderful land of folk-lore. But there is yet one more mention of Arthur in history, in the pages of William of Malmesbury's *Gesta Regum*, written in the early years of the twelfth century. William describes Ambrosius as king of the Britons and Arthur as his general. William had no room for the legends that had by then grown up round the name of the general— he thought them nonsense—but he believed in Arthur as a person.

On the death of Vortigern, the strength of the Britons grew faint, their diminished hopes went backwards ; and straightway they would have come to ruin, had not Ambrosius, the sole survivor of the Romans, who was monarch of the realm after Vortigern, repressed the over-weening barbarians through the distinguished achievements of the war-like Arthur. This is that Arthur of whom the trifling of the Britons talk such nonsense even to-day ; a man clearly worthy not to be dreamed in fallacious fables, but to be proclaimed in veracious histories as one who long sustained his tottering country, and gave the shattered minds of his fellow-citizens an edge for war. Finally at the siege of Mount Badon, relying upon the image of the Mother of the Lord, which he had sewn upon his armour, he made single-handed upon nine hundred of the enemy, and routed them with incredible slaughter.

William may not hold with legends, but he perpetuates one ! Samson and the Philistines, Thor, Hercules—the story is really the same, the causes the same too.   Even so, William was a serious historian—very different from Geoffrey of Monmouth, who a few years later produced his *Historia Regum Britanniæ*. This astonishing mixture of chronicle, fable, romance and poetry is supposed to be a history of Britain from the time of Brutus to that of Cadwallader.   It is crammed full of mistakes and distortions, it is obviously highly coloured by the imagination of the writer, but it appeared in an age of romance and it leapt to popularity.   It glorified Arthur in no mean manner, removing him altogether from the realm of history, and it has been drawn upon by every subsequent writer who has dealt with the subject.   From Geoffrey on- wards we deal with the Arthur of folk-lore.   Wace, Chretien de Troyes, Marie de France, Layamon, Malory, Tennyson, all make use of old ballads, quite a few of which have nothing to do with Arthur at all (the legend of the Holy Grail had nothing to do with Arthur in its original form, nor had the Round Table) but all of which were incorporated.   So now the man has gone, and we are left with the sleeping hero (even the alleged discovery of the grave at Glastonbury— which came at a financial crisis in the history of the monastery, a most opportune discovery—did not kill that belief), with the Round Table and Lancelot and all, with Guinevere (Giraldus, by the way, is the only writer who mentions that Guinevere was Arthur's second wife), with the undying legend.

And so far as Amesbury is concerned it is only the legend that matters.   For many people Guinevere is Amesbury. They may never have heard of Ambrosius, after whom the town is named ;   they may care little for Arthur and dismiss the Knights of the Round Table as a pleasant tale for children ; but they know that it was here that Guinevere took the veil, when Arthur died, that it was here that Lancelot found her dead and bore her across the downs a matter of thirty miles to lie beside her husband at Glastonbury.   It has become almost a " local girl " story.   Mention that Guinevere is but

the Welsh Gwenhwyvar, and that there is a rhyme about her
in Wales :

> Gwenhwyvar, the daughter of Gogyrvan the Giant,
> Bad when little, worse when great.

and they will look at you as though you were a blasphemer
and a bad smell. You may know all this—the Welsh legends
and the Scottish no less than the English—and yet, in Amesbury, it is difficult not to believe.

I found myself sitting in a little café, drinking coffee, and
thinking hard about Arthur and Guinevere and Lancelot and
the rest :

> When Queen Guinevere understood that King Arthur
> was slain and all the noble knights, Sir Mordred and all
> the remnant, then the Queen stole away, and five ladies
> with her, and so she went to Almesbury ; and there she
> let make herself a nun and wore white clothes and black,
> and great penance she took, as ever did sinful lady in this
> land, and never creature could make her merry ; but lived
> in fasting, prayers and alms deeds, that all manner of
> people marvelled how virtuously she was changed. Now
> leave we Queen Guinevere in Almesbury, a nun in white
> clothes and black, and there she was Abbess and ruler as
> reason would ; and turn we from her and speak we of
> Sir Lancelot du Lake.

Sir Lancelot was at Dover Castle, I remembered, when he
heard of the death of the King :

> I will myself ride and seek my lady Queen Guinevere,
> for as I hear say she hath had great pain and much disease ;
> and I heard say she is fled into the west. . . .
> So he departed and rode westerly, and there he sought
> a seven or eight days and at last he came to a nunnery,
> and there was Queen Guinevere ware of Sir Lancelot as
> he walked in the cloister. And when she saw him there
> she swooned thrice that all the ladies and gentlewomen
> had work enough to hold the Queen up.

But they parted, for she insisted :

> for all the love that was betwixt us that thou never see me more in this visage ; and I command thee in God's behalf, that thou forsake my company and to thy kingdom thou turn again, for as well as I have loved thee, mine heart will not serve me to see thee again . . . therefore, Sir Lancelot, go to thy realm, and there take thee a wife, and live with her with joy and bliss.

Sir Lancelot does not. Looking his last upon her living, there in the cloister at Amesbury, he swears to become a monk even as she had become a nun. He goes to a hermitage where the Archbishop of Canterbury was, and after a penance of six years, he took the habit. But after but a year

> upon a night there came a vision to Sir Lancelot, and charged him in remission of his sins to hasten him to Almesbury. " And when thou come there thou shalt find Queen Guinevere dead. And therefore take thy fellows with thee and purvey them of an horse-bier, and fetch thou the corpse of her and bury her by her husband, the noble King Arthur." Then Sir Lancelot rose on a day, and took his eight fellows with him and on foot they yede from Glastonbury to Almesbury, the which is little more than thirty miles. And thither they came within two days for they were weak and feeble to go. And when Sir Lancelot was come to Almesbury within the nunnery, Queen Guinevere died but half an hour afore. And the ladies told Sir Lancelot that Queen Guinevere told them all as she passed, that Sir Lancelot had been priest near a twelvemonth, and hither he cometh as fast as he may to fetch my corpse ; and beside my lord King Arthur he shall bury me. Wherefore the Queen said in hearing of them all : I beseech Almighty God that I may never have power to see Sir Lancelot with my worldly eyes ; and this, said all the ladies, was ever her prayer these two days, till she was dead. Then Sir Lancelot saw her visage, but he wept not greatly, but sighed. And so he did all the

observances of the service himself both the *dirige* and on
the morn he sang Mass. And there was ordained a
horse-bier; and so with a hundred torches burning ever
about the corpse of the Queen, and ever Sir Lancelot with
his eight fellows went about the horse-bier, singing and
reading many an holy orison, and frankincense upon the
corpse incensed. Thus Sir Lancelot and his eight fellows
went on foot from Almesbury to Glastonbury. And when
they were come to the chapel and the hermitage, there
she has a *dirige* with great devotion. And on the morrow
the hermit that sometime was Bishop of Canterbury sang
the Mass of Requiem with great devotion. And Sir
Lancelot was the first that offered, and then also his eight
fellows. And then she was wrapped in cered cloth of
Raines, from top to toe, in thirty fold; and after she was
put in a web of lead, and then in a coffin of marble. And
when she was put in the earth Sir Lancelot swooned and
lay long still, while the hermit came and awaked him and
said: ye be to blame for ye displease God with such
manner of sorrow-making. Truly said Sir Lancelot, I
trust I do not displease God for He knoweth the manner
of mine intent. For my sorrow was not, nor is not, for
any rejoicing of sin, but my sorrow may never have end.
For when I remember her beauty, and of her noblesse,
that was both with her king and with her, so when I saw
her corpse and his corpse so lie together, truly my heart
would not serve to sustain my careful body. Also I
remember me how by my default, my orgule, and my
pride, that they were both laid full low, that were peerless
that ever was living of Christian people; wit you well,
said Sir Lancelot, this remembered, of her kindness and
my unkindness, sank so to my heart that I might not
sustain myself.

There may never have been a Sir Lancelot du Lake. It
does not matter. That there was a Gwenhwyvar is, I think,
beyond doubt. Whether she was Queen or wanton, or both,
does not matter. Here is one of the great love stories of the

world. No matter how many times you read it, no matter how well you know it, you cannot fail to be moved by it.

And you can think what you like about the probability or otherwise of the characters. At least there was a nunnery here at Amesbury as early as the sixth century. True all we really know of it is contained in the story of Lancelot and Guinevere, and that is also the last we know of it. But we do know that Amesbury was a holy place. Ambrosius may not have been born here, but he was buried here. And it was here, after the battle of Maisbeli, that he buried the bodies of the Romano-British nobles who had been killed. He would not have done so had not the place already been famous and holy. Moreover, tradition links Amesbury with Glastonbury as one of the earliest centres of Christianity in England. The Welsh Triads mention Amesbury as one of the three great centres established in the early days of the Christian era—the other two were Llan Iltud Vaur in Glamorganshire and Glastonbury. It is a likely place for early Christianity anyhow, for it is hard by Stonehenge, and the Christian missionaries had a shrewd fondness for building their churches close to centres of pagan worship. Once, no doubt, as at Glastonbury, there was a monastery as well as a nunnery. In Lancelot's time there was only the nunnery left, and that was approaching its end. All, or most of, the country to the east was either under the domination of Saxon pagans or threatened by them—surely for no other reason would an Archbishop of Canterbury have been in hermitage at Glastonbury?—and Glastonbury in the marsh was a safer resting place for the body of the Queen than this town on the river up which Saxon invaders were soon to make their way. The appearance in the story of this hermit Archbishop seems to me to be entirely credible. It is not the sort of thing that even the imaginative Geoffrey would have made up on his own. It is of no value to the story itself. It is the relic of tradition, a ghost from the troubled past. Lancelot may not have existed—though I should be surprised indeed to find that Guinevere had not a lover—but that fugitive Archbishop did.

Amesbury shortly fell to the Saxons, and possibly was totally destroyed. Yet there was once a Saxon church here, for carved Saxon stones have been found on the site of the present church. But of all that we know little. The new Amesbury on the site of the old was built by Ethelfrida in 980 as part of the expiation for her sin in murdering her son-in-law. It was a convent she built, of course, but as was inevitable a town soon grew up around it. The convent lasted for just two hundred years, but in 1177 the evil lives of the Abbess and her nuns became a little too much to wink at any longer. The nuns were distributed round other convents (probably taking their appetites with them) and the Abbess was turned loose to do as she would (evidently she was regarded as past redemption) and once more Amesbury fell to nonentity.

Not for very long, however. Within a couple of years the convent was given to the king's favourite abbey of Fontevrault in Anjou, and from there a prioress and twenty-four nuns were sent to Amesbury. And so was born the greatest of all the female houses of England. In fact, of course, it was a mixed house—men and women—but the chief was the Abbess and all the law and ordering of it and its property was in the hands of women. It soon became famous throughout England. The list of Royal ladies who were humble nuns is a formidable one; the great lodged here on their way through to London; kings visited it; nobles were born in it. And so it flourished until Henry VIII ran short of money and ordered its Dissolution.

But this time Amesbury was not to sink forgotten. There was Webb to build a great house from the design of Inigo Jones (it was rebuilt in 1840), there was Gay who wrote here his *Beggar's Opera*, there was a delightful Duchess of Queensberry.

> Thus Kitty, beautiful and young
> And mild as colt untamed
> Bespoke the fair from whence she sprung
> With little rage inflamed;

Inflamed with rage at sad restraint
  Which wise mamma ordained,
And sorely vexed to play the saint
  Whilst wit and beauty reigned.

" Shall I thumb holy books, confined
  With Abigail, forsaken ?
Kitty's for other things designed
  Or I am much mistaken.

" Must Lady Jenny frisk about
  And visit with her cousins ?
At balls must she make all the rout
  And bring home hearts by dozens ?

" What has she better, pray, than I ?
  What hidden charms to boast,
That all mankind for her should die
  Whilst I am scarce a toast ?

" Dearest mamma, for once let me
  Unchained my future try,
I'll have my Earl as well as she
  Or know the reason why."

Fondness prevailed—mamma gave way,
  Kitty at heart's desire
Obtained the chariot for a day
  And set the world on fire.

So Prior sang. Set the world on fire, she did ; but I
doubt if she was happy. She made her life so full that I
cannot help but think she did so in order that she might not
have time to think.

All this goes through your mind when you visit Amesbury.
The place is full of atmosphere, full of character. And this
despite the fact that there is little left that is old save only the
beautiful but mutilated church of St. Mary and St. Melor
(what that Cornish saint is doing here I cannot think) which
may have been the church of the great convent. It is a large
cruciform building with a low central tower, singularly
massive, so that it looks much squatter than it really is. The

nave is Norman, built of flint, and you can still see where the old round-headed windows were blocked up. The rest is mainly Early English. Once I imagine that it must have been one of the loveliest Early English churches in the country. But it was restored in 1907, and this and an earlier restoration by Butterworth in the middle of the nineteenth century have removed any loveliness there once was. Now it is interesting, but gloomy. There is about it something of the dignity of a cathedral, but there is also a severity that I find quite overwhelming. I was glad to get out into the rain and Amesbury again.

I have called Amesbury a town. That seems natural. In fact it is no more than a large village—indeed there are many larger villages in the country—but the dignity of its Georgian buildings belong to a town rather than a village. Its importance, too, though long since past gives to it that dignity. Roads meet here—the Andover road joins that from Marlborough and that also from Mere—and the river seems suddenly to have swelled. It is, in its quiet little way, a downland capital, lying in a bowl—a village in size, but a town in all else.

Once it was a great place for the making of clay pipes. Time was when a pipe-smoker cherished his " Amesbury ". They do not make clay pipes here now—who smokes a clay now anyway ?—and I could not find anyone who remembered when the last one was made hereabouts, though it could not have been so very long ago. But my enquiries led me to a bed. I had begun to get a little worried about this. The rain was steady and heavy and it had been going on for so long that there was little chance of finding anywhere dry, unless I could get into a shed. But search of Amesbury had failed to show a suitable shed that could be entered without breaking, and I had almost resigned myself to an uncomfortable night in a public telephone box (I have slept in one before now, but I do not recommend them—very cold and very cramped) when I got into conversation in a doorway with an old man about these clay pipes. His wife would put me up for the night, he said, and took me to a small cottage.

The bed was feather and comfortable, and porridge in the morning was excellent. The charge was four shillings, and this included drying my clothes, which were sodden. There is much kindness yet to be found in England.

## CHAPTER III

## TO SALISBURY

Iᴛ had stopped raining in the morning. The skies looked heavy and full, but the wind had gone round to the east, and it seemed like a fine morning at least. Stonehenge is not on the river, but what matter? It would be foolish to visit Amesbury and not Stonehenge, and anyway the Avenue had once run from the Circle to the river and that was excuse enough if any were needed.

I think that Stonehenge disappoints most people when first they see it. There are so many pictures of it, and you hear such a lot about the size of it and the hugeness of its stones, and then you come over the crest of the rise—in a car probably—and there it is before you, quite a distance away and a little below you, and it looks small, and brownish-grey and anything but imposing. The plain is so huge and empty, and the sky illimitable, as wide as the world. In fact, of course, it is a miracle that it stands at all, an even greater miracle that it stands in something like suitable isolation. Once, indeed, military buildings almost ringed it round. They have gone now, and it is properly cared for by the State, and little stone pillars have been put up where great stones used to stand, so that you can see pretty well what the whole plan was.

And there is a spell about Stonehenge. You might not think so when you see it for the first time, banded on either side by the blue-grey ribbon of main roads, and with that glaring white car-park and the little pay-box. But as you walk towards it, it grows, and the stones do become huge, and the roads fade away, and the noise of the traffic dies, and, suddenly, you are in a temple, and you are very small and isolated. Stonehenge startles and subdues.

NEAR BODENHAM AND LINGFORD CASTLE

DOWNTON BRIDGE

The human significance is there, as eloquent as the ruins of a castle. But the fashioning of it, the thoughts and the motives that conceived it, are so remote, so far removed from anything that we can understand. We can understand a little about the Romans, the Saxons, the Normans, but this —this belongs to the blank in history. We may marvel at the magic which conveyed from afar and reared up these mighty stones—and we do marvel, we cannot help doing so —but the physical side of that presents little difficulty. All the largest stones are sarsen, and at the very furthest they came from the Marlborough Downs. The other stones came from the Prescelly Hills in Pembrokeshire, far away on the rim of Wales, but they are comparatively small stones, and the difficulty of bringing them here to this bare spot on the chalk would not have been much of a problem to a people talented to plan so great a monument as this.

It is that word, Plan, that makes Stonehenge the fascinating problem that it is. It is marvellous enough just to look at it; the stones immense enough, the site inspiring enough. You cannot look and not be impressed. But you can look without thinking. It is when you begin to think about it and what it all means that the thing hits you. Planned it obviously was, and carefully sited : but what for, why just like this ?

In the car-park when I reached Stonehenge on this morning was an enormous American car—one of those ultra-modern cars in which it is so hard to tell the front from the back at first glance—and there was a flag on the bonnet, and all sorts of badges and crests, a large official car. In the back there was a very fat man in a light grey suit fast asleep. Within the circle I came upon his family—a small, perky, smartly-dressed wife, a very pretty cool daughter also smartly dressed, with the wide mouth and friendly smile so characteristic of modern American girlhood, and a tall loose-limbed young man, armed with the inevitable Leica. It was too early in the morning for the usual crowds of sightseers, and there was only one Ministry of Works official in smart blue uniform about. I put my rucksack on the ground and prepared to look around once again. Almost immediately the mother was on to me, plying me with questions, and searching at the same time in a guide-book, which I thought was a little unfair. Did I think this? Did I think that? There used to be human sacrifices here in the Druid times, didn't there? No, I said, I didn't think there used. And anyway, I said, I didn't think that the Druids had anything to do with Stonehenge. They preferred oak groves, I said. "Say, now, you have disappointed Ma," said the daughter, giving me a very nice smile; "there's nothing Ma likes so much as a little human sacrifice, and she's mad keen on your Druids." "Well, I'm sorry," I said, "but really I don't think they had anything to do with this place. And really I don't think that there was ever any human sacrifice here. She ought to come on Midsummer's Day. She'll see plenty of modern Druids doing their stuff then." A rash remark that, for I then had to give a full description of what did happen on Midsummer's Night, and though I have been I do not really know what happens. But soon she was back to the attack.

"This is the Altar Stone, isn't it?" she asked, prodding with her foot.

"Yes," I said.

"Well, then," she crowed triumphantly, "what did they have that for if not sacrifices?"

"I'm sure I don't know," I said. "You see, we call it the Altar Stone. But we weren't here at the time, and we don't really know what it was. It might have been something quite different from that."

"But wasn't this place planned as a sort of sundial?" she asked.

"Orientated, you mean, Ma," said her daughter. "Wasn't it orientated to catch the sun just at sunrise on Midsummer's Morning on this Altar Stone?"

"I don't know," I said. "I know that that is supposed roughly to be the idea. But I don't know."

"But you don't think so," said the daughter, acutely.

"No, I don't," I said. And Mother sat down abruptly

on a stone, and said, " My, these English—always wrecking their traditions, and they're so proud of them too."

But was Stonehenge so planned ?

That it was planned is obvious : it did not just grow up haphazard like an English town. If you come to it along the Avenue from the river Avon, a distance of one and a half miles, as I did on this morning, you get, I think, a better idea of the whole. The Avenue (though this is not evident for the whole of its course nowadays to a man on foot, although I understand that it can be seen from an aeroplane) is enclosed between two parallel banks and ditches. It was obviously a main road in the days when Stonehenge was busy. It leads to the north-east side of the whole structure and there is just a single entrance. Stonehenge itself is roughly circular, the boundary being a low bank and a shallow ditch. Inside this there is a great circle of empty socket-holes, known as the Aubrey Holes because they were first noted by the seventeenth-century antiquary. There is then a considerable space, and then two more rings of socket-holes, known as the Y and Z holes. Then you come to the great outer circle of sarsen stones, incomplete now but once lintelled to form a continuous ring. Inside this is a circle of bluestone monoliths, and inside this inner ring there is a double horse-shoe—the outer formed of five tremendous trilithons (pairs of lintelled monoliths of sarsen), the inner of small bluestone monoliths. And there, lying across the toe of this inner bluestone horse-shoe, is the apparent centrepiece of the whole thing, a great recumbent slab, known as the Altar Stone, which was brought here either from Glamorgan or Milford Haven. There are a few outlying stones, and one of these, known as the Hele Stone, is situated at the head of the Avenue. If you stand by the Altar Stone and look back along the axis of the horse-shoes to the Hele Stone at the head of the Avenue, you will be facing the point where the sun will rise on Midsummer's Day.

It is all very wonderful. It is wonderful enough without worrying about that Midsummer's Day bit. Here, at Stone-henge, the peak of architectural refinement—at least for the prehistoric west—was attained. The transverse slabs that made the outer ring of sarsens continuous were not only curved lengthwise to fit the circumference of the circle, but they grow broader towards the top to counteract the fore-shortening when viewed from the ground. And they are secured (as are the cross slabs of the trilithons) by mortices hollowed out to fit over tenons projecting from the tops of the uprights. It must have taken a great length of time to do with the primitive instruments the workmen had available. The force that moved this tremendous work, that brought stones all the way from distant Wales—a matter of at least 200 miles (transport in prehistoric Britain must have been better organized than we realize)—was vital indeed.

It was not all done at once, of course. The circular bank and ditch, the Avenue, and the Aubrey Holes are much earlier than the rest of the monument. In other words Stonehenge originally consisted just of a causeway leading to a circular bank and ditch within which was a circle of upright timber posts. The sarsen ring and the sarsen horse-shoe were the next to be set up, and last of all the bluestones were erected, evidently as part of the same scheme (though it seems that originally they stood in the Aubrey Holes).

The original work—the bank and ditch and the Aubrey Holes—was planned from a different centre from the rest of the work. It is also evident that the bluestone circle and horse-shoe, which are rather irregular in plan, had to evade some obstruction that is no longer there. How long it all took no one knows, but it is certain that there was an over-whelming conviction behind it all, a religion that was a real driving force. It was not Druidism, which was a Celtic religion and very much later, but it is highly probable that Celtic priests made use of Stonehenge towards the end, in just the same way as Christian priests made use of pagan sites.

But was the whole monument orientated for the sun's rise on Midsummer Day? Was it an astronomical instrument? I do not think there can be any doubt at all that the original building—the circular bank and ditch and the Aubrey ring—was not. But what of the rest?

This idea (of precise alignment, of Stonehenge as an astronomical instrument) is quite new. I do not think that it is more than one hundred years old or so. I think that it is important to realize that : that it is the idea of modern man, with all modern man's advantages. Someone got the idea, and there was this ancient structure and the structure could be fitted to the idea. It is not very difficult to make existing facts fit ideas. That they do fit, does not necessarily mean that the idea is correct.

I am not an astronomer. I am not an archæologist. I have, therefore, no right to express myself on this extremely intricate subject, which is a combination of the two sciences, and I am well aware that I am exposing myself to attack from men well qualified to rip me to pieces. But it does seem to me, from what I have read, that all too frequently common-sense has been pushed firmly into the background in order that this or that favourite theory may have freedom of movement. You can take one fact and build up on it the most marvellous edifice of theory. People have been doing that with Stonehenge for years and years.

I think that it was Sir Norman Lockyer who started it all. It is a fact that the causeway of approach, the avenue, and the stones of Stonehenge are so arranged that they face towards the north-east, and, moreover, towards that northerly point on the horizon at which the sun rises at midsummer. That is a fact. From it has been built a theory, very widely held to-day and due originally to Lockyer, that Stonehenge was a temple of sun-worship. But, so far as I know (and I have read a good deal about this, everything that I can lay hands on that is not too complex and technical for me to understand) there is absolutely no evidence that there was at any time any organized institutional sun-worship in Britain. For that matter I know of no evidence at all that Stonehenge (or any other stone circle) was used at any time as a place for public worship of the sun or anything else. Conjecture is not evidence. It seems pretty certain that Avebury and Stonehenge were temples—and I believe myself that they were—but we do not *know* for certain that they were.

Popular tradition has it that on the longest day of the year the sun, if you stand within the interior of Stonehenge and watch it from there, rises exactly over the Hele Stone. That is why it is a temple of sun-worship, of course! Lockyer is, I believe, responsible for the idea; he stood within Stonehenge and watched. But it is absolutely certain that the sun did not rise over the Hele Stone from the direction chosen by Lockyer, and that it will not do so at midsummer for just about 500 years!

And then, what do you mean by sunrise? Sunrise is not just something that happens in a flash, and is over. Astronomically, I understand, the moment of sunrise is that moment when the disc of the sun is cut in half by the true horizon. But you might say that sunrise was the moment when the first gleam appears. Or you might say that it was the moment when the whole disc of the sun first showed clear of the horizon. Which you chose would make quite a difference to positions on the ground.

The whole thing becomes even more difficult when you try to fix the date of Stonehenge by the sun. This is a favourite pastime of large numbers of people, and it is true that if Stonehenge is really aligned as an astronomical instrument, then you should be able to fix the date of its construction pretty accurately. Now, it is true that if you draw a straight line between the two uprights of the central and tallest arch to the centre of the circle it will cut the Altar Stone at right angles, and if you then prolong it it will run almost centrally down the Avenue and cut the horizon on Lark Hill just at the point where the sun rises on Midsummer's Day—that is, if you are standing on the south-west of the circle and looking to the north-east. You will then (weather permitting) see the rising sun framed between the uprights. But it will *not* rise over the Hele Stone. On the other hand, if you go to Stonehenge with the midsummer crowd and get a good position with your back to the end of the great stone (known as No. 55) you will see (weather permitting) the sun rise exactly over the Hele Stone. But then you will *not* be on the axis of Stonehenge. And then, of course, much depends on the eye-level of the observer—a man of six feet will see these things from a slightly different position (slight but very important) from a man of five feet six inches. That, and which part of the process of sunrise you take as being *the* moment, makes a difference of thousands of years to the date. And again, it matters tremendously which eye you use. It does not matter where you stand, looking down the line between stones 30 and 1 (the middle point between those stones is the only point that can be taken on the true axis of Stonehenge) the difference between the position of your right eye and your left makes a difference of 500 years in the date ! And any slight movement of the head, say five inches either way, will make a difference of about 2,000 years. As an astronomical instrument I cannot believe in Stonehenge—too much rests on human frailty. As a temple of sun-worship I cannot believe in it at all—did short high-priests stand on chairs or the shoulders of their fellows, did tall ones kneel down ? As a means of fixing the date of construction I just cannot swallow it at all. If you stand at the point at which Lockyer stood in 1901 and take the half-risen sun as the moment then I believe that the date would be 3500 B.C. as near as makes no difference. But if you stood in the same position and took the fully-risen sun as the moment then I believe that the date would be 5200 B.C. or thereabouts. But I understand that archæologists, working from another standpoint altogether, are more or less agreed that 2000 B.C. is about the date, and there are some who maintain that that date is too early.

But, I think, that if Stonehenge was deliberately orientated at all, it might have been done as a way of fixing a date in an agricultural calendar. Not one single day, but a week. The single day would not matter at all. The difference between the longest day and the previous day and the following day is only a matter of a few seconds anyhow. At midsummer, at the latitude of Greenwich, the sun rises at 3.44 a.m. and (omitting the seconds) continues to do so for about a week and then rises later. Sunrise time ending sees the beginning of a fixed period of sunset time at the same latitude. No matter how much the builders of Stonehenge knew about astronomy, they could not have been capable of the minute calculations necessary to work out all this. They did not moreover know anything about leap years. Midsummer Day is not a fixed date. The longest day and the shortest day fall later year by year, and it is only leap year that brings them back to the starting point. I believe that in one hundred years (a mathematician has worked it out for me) the date of the longest day would move forward by two days, from June 20th to June 22nd. The builders of Stonehenge would not know anything about that either. And why should they bother? All they had got to do was to observe the points of sunrise, and note the point where it changed less and less each day—it would change very little for some three weeks at one point on the horizon in summer—and, if they wished, they could mark that point. But they would not have to build a Stonehenge to do so : a couple of stones or a couple of earth mounds would do quite as well. Very clever men designed and built Stonehenge— that is evident—but I do not think we need make them cleverer than they were. They could have got all they wanted to know about the sun's position without building Stone- henge, and without the aid of instruments such as modern astronomers use.

Stonehenge is orientated to the north-east. There is no doubt about that. But whether that orientation is deliberate or not is another matter. All probability suggests that it was deliberately so placed, but it might not have been. It is easy to see now—when someone has pointed it out—but what exactly the builders were after must remain a matter of conjecture. And, if it was deliberately so planned, then it must have taken a very long time indeed. One year's observa- tion of the sun's movements would not have been sufficient, nor two years. And anyone who has watched the sun rise at midsummer on Salisbury Plain will know that there are rather more days on which you do not see it rise than there are on which you do.

The monument is there, grand and simple and so impressive. It stands a perpetual challenge to theorists. But conjecture is not fact. It is very good fun. But it is not fact.

All this I tried to tell my American acquaintances. They listened very politely. We tried angles, we sat down and lay down, and squinted. The boy must have been about six feet four inches, whereas I am only just six feet with a stretch : the mother may have been five feet two (though I should doubt it), the daughter about five feet six or so. There was plenty of scope for proving that you do not see things from the same angle if you are of different heights. There is never much ice to break with Americans, and we had a most enjoyable morning scrambling round these great stones. But it was the girl who alone got the feeling of the place. Suddenly she said : " My God, this must be terrifying in the dark of a winter's night and you all by yourself." Her mother and her brother looked at her in amazement. The idea that anyone should come out here by themselves on a winter's night struck them as silly. But the thought sobered her. She was silent for quite a while.

And I knew how she felt. I have spent a November night at Stonehenge, and more than one summer night, alone. Midsummer Night is quite another matter. You might as well be on Blackpool promenade then. But alone in November, and a mist swirling a few inches from the ground, distorting everything, bringing the great grey stones to life ; the rise of the wind across the plain, so that you can hear its voice in the grasses long before it hits you ; the whisper of rain on the stone. All those things you can experience elsewhere of a November night. But here at Stonehenge, they are different, more compelling. It is hard not to believe that there is life about you. And in summer, with a nightjar calling, and the lights flashing on the roads, and the sweet distant wailing of the stone curlew—it is harder still then. You can have done with conjecture then. There is more locked away in these stones than mere history. There are all the secrets of a great people of whom we know nothing at all. And the place is filled with their presence still, when darkness falls.

The boy looked at his watch. "Ma," he said, "Pop ought to have slept it off by now. We'd better be getting back."

I walked over to my rucksack, and heaved it on my back. It interested them. Where was I going? All the usual questions. Well, I was going to Christchurch in the end, but at the moment back to Amesbury. Could they give me a lift? But I wanted to get on to the road that runs along the riverside, and that could be reached easily by walking a mere mile across country, and it would be easier for me too. They pressed a huge hunk of chocolate on me, when they heard that I did not know where I would be for luncheon, and then went off to wake up Pop. I wondered what it was he was sleeping off.

A considerable area round Stonehenge is now National Trust property. Even without that, even allowing for the encroachment of the military, the plain about Stonehenge is still reasonably wild and deserted. Amesbury, a couple of miles away to the south-east, is hidden in the valley of the Avon behind the wooded height of Vespasian's Camp. (Needless to say, this is not a Roman encampment and there is no evidence at all that Vespasian was ever here.) There is turf all the way across the horizon, turf all the way to the skyline, turf thickly dotted with the grave mounds of the distant dead—long barrows, bell barrows, bowl barrows, disc barrows, barrows from the dim past to the Roman period and perhaps even later, for the Saxons used this grave form too at times. I daresay you could get together a nice theory about these barrows and the way they are sited, if you took the trouble—and no doubt someone has—but it is much better, I feel, just to notice them and to enjoy the walking on close springy turf. There were a lot of rooks about this morning, and a few starlings and jackdaws, and they moved in front of me like a flock of black sheep, until I had driven them a certain distance, and then they would get up and fly over my head and behind me, and start again. Time and again it happened, as though each party knew when it had reached the end of its grazing ground, and must go no further for the feeding belonged to other parties. As soon as one group of birds had flown back to start again, there was another group moving along in front, walking or taking short flights, and so it was all the way down to the Avon. There were some hares, too, but not nearly so many as I had seen on the other side of the valley, but there were more rabbits, scampering about just in the manner of hares, and recking little of cover.

The Avon after its huge bend and many divisions at Amesbury takes on a different character. A chalk stream still, it has now a gravelly appearance, running smoothly in runnels, a very fishable-looking water. And all the while now it is dividing and joining up and dividing again, just like a real trout stream in Hampshire. It does not make the walking of it any the easier—and, more times than I like to think about now, I was driven back on to the road. Still, from the road you get a better view of it all than you do from the actual bank, though you cannot of course see the fish. I spent some time lying on my tummy looking at a fat pike (which should have had no business in a good trout water at this time of year) lying almost on the bottom, tail gently moving, and eyes fixed on the stream above him. I watched him for many minutes and in all that time he did not move a muscle save for the gentle movement of the tail, and nothing came over him. But patience, I have no doubt, was in due course rewarded. Further down stream again I watched a water vole for a few moments chasing its tail just in the manner of a kitten, running round and round on the bottom of a shallow reach, and every now and then coming straight up to the surface and just breaking it with its nose—sufficient, obviously, to get a breath—and then returning to its game or its exercise.

It is seven miles by the main road from Amesbury to Old Sarum, a high bare road, lonely save for the lorries and the motor-cars, which runs by High Post Corner and the golf course. By the side road it is about a mile longer. But this road, which is the older, goes through some pleasant little villages and hamlets and is never lonely though it

carries much less traffic. The first of these little villages is
Durnford, below Ogbury Camp. The manor house here
once belonged to the Hungerfords and it was here that
Evelyn came in 1654. "Dined at a ferme of my Uncle
Hungerford's called Darneford Magna, situate in a valley
under ye plaine most sweetly watered abounding in trouts
catched by speare in ye nighte, when they came attracted by
a light set in ye sterne of a boate." There are still plenty of
trout, for I saw them. But nowadays that method of fishing
is not much practised, being frowned upon by the purists.
I have tried it myself, but without success, but I have watched
experts at it (on this very stream, too, but not on this actual
water) and very effective it is when the man behind the spear
is an expert. I cannot say that I have watched a man perform
from a boat on one of these small chalk streams—that would
be too risky in these strait-laced days—but the result is the
same from the bank ; indeed, I suspect that it is rather more
effective from the bank, for that is solid and immovable
whereas a boat has an unpleasant habit of rocking at the
critical moment. There are more ways than one of catching
a trout, and it has always struck me as a pity that men con-
centrate so much on the dry fly.

But the delight of Durnford for me is the church (that
would be so even had I been able to fish) which is small and
old, just a nave with north and south porches and a chancel
and a western tower. There is Norman work in the north
and south doorways, the latter framed in oak of the fifteenth
century. There is Norman work, too, in the chancel arch,
which has its pillars delightfully carved with birds. The
birds are of a later date, and the man who worked them was
a real craftsman, and one, moreover, who knew his birds.
I do not mean by that that you can at this date (for the carving
is at the latest early thirteenth century) recognize the species
at a glance or even at all (though I think that you can make
a good guess at some of them) but I do mean that the carver
knew what a bird looked like and how it moved. These
are no mere scribblings in stone. Some of the chancel work
is restoration of the late nineteenth century—quite tastefully

done—but much of it is still late twelfth century, the slight pointed lancet windows, for example, though those on the north side have unfortunately been blocked. The east window, which is a triple lancet under a pointed arch, is of the same date. The windows of the nave are fifteenth century, but the roof is of the late thirteenth so I think, though so great an authority as Ponting put it at one hundred years earlier. There is a very lovely font of the early twelfth century with some excellent sculpturing at its base. But the real joy of this little church is the tower, a thirteenth-century structure that is almost perfect and a noble sight indeed.

There is a catalogue of Durnford church. Not in any really noteworthy way different from the catalogue that could be made out for many a little village church in this country, for many a village church in this county for that matter. It is not age, nor is it lack of size, that makes this church so delightful. It is not, as a matter of fact, those things that make any church attractive. They are interesting to look at, to study, they satisfy a certain historical longing that is powerful in many of us, but they do not win us by these things. It is personality that wins. And Durnford church is full of it. It has what is missing from ninety-nine out of every hundred churches these days—a homely welcoming atmosphere. It seems lived in and warm. I got the feeling that people really did worship in it, not just go to it out of a sense of duty, or because the vicar expected it, or to show off a new hat to jealous and less fortunate citizens. Whatever it is that gives a church this atmosphere, I do not know, but Durnford had it so strongly that I spent much too long in it. I ate my chocolate and wandered about and sat down and drank it all in, and enjoyed it more than I have enjoyed a church for a long while. And when I came out it was raining again.

It was raining hard, harder than it had the previous evening and it did not look at all as though it intended to stop. Again the Downs on the far side of the narrow valley were hidden by the grey sheet, and they are a good deal higher there on the east bank than here on the west. That is a bad sign anyway, for it means that there is no lift to the rain and no wind with it either. Indeed I could see no clouds at all—the whole sky was one vast cloud. Not much good pottering around the bends of this river here I thought, and I set out along the road to eat up the five miles into Salisbury. Actually the stream keeps very close to the road all the way, often right alongside it, and so, rain or no, I got a good view of it, all the way to Avon Bridge just below Old Sarum. And here, the rain eased sufficiently to make me think that after all I would cross and go to see the old town before I made my way into Salisbury.

Old Sarum from below looks grim and desolate and dominant. When Cobbett arrived here he shook his fist at it and called it " the accursed hill ". Why I do not know, but from below it has that sort of look about it. It does not look a friendly place.

Here once was a great Roman station, Sorbiodunum, and the junction of six great roads. I am aware that this view is not held by some authorities—and I am no authority—and that these authorities believe that the Roman Sorbiodunum was a little further to the west at Stratford-sub-Castle. But, even though that site would be much more advantageously placed for water, it is in every other way less suitable, and I cannot believe that, despite the few Roman remains that were found during excavation (there were some), this was not the site of the Roman station. It was not, of course, ever a station of the size or importance of Winchester or Silchester or Dorchester or Cirencester, but it was certainly the most important point between Winchester and any of those places. It was never a town in Roman times, so much as a fort, a garrison, an important strategic place covering very important lines of communication. Even during the height of the Roman occupation of Britain, such garrison strongholds must have been needed, not because of the danger of revolt but merely for the proper and easeful functioning of police work.

This hill, rising three hundred feet above the river valley— a projecting spur of Salisbury Plain really—was inhabited before the Romans came, of course. The original ramparts were Neolithic. Tracks met here before the great roads were laid down. The place was always of great strategic importance. Despite the paucity of Roman remains, it is impossible to believe that the Romans would not have made use of such a site. For that matter Saxon remains have proved to be few and far between, and yet the place is reputed to have been of considerable importance in Saxon times.

The Saxons called it Sarisbyrig. According to the Saxon Chronicle Cynric captured Sarisbyrig from the Britons in 552. There can be no doubt whatever that Sarisbyrig was somewhere in this neighbourhood, and if it was not on the site of what is now known as Old Sarum it is difficult to see where it could have been. It is true that the Saxons did not like hill-top settlements and settled in the valleys, leaving the Romano-British hill towns deserted, and this coupled with the paucity of Saxon remains has been taken by some authorities to show that the Saxons were never settled in Old Sarum. But it should be remembered that Cynric was invading a Romano-British country, and the towns he would attack would be hill towns, for the British had a liking for them in preference to settlements in the valleys. The Sarisbyrig that Cynric captured would have been a hill-top town and I do not think it reasonable to deny that the place was Old Sarum. Thereafter, the Saxons lived at Sarisbyrig. There can be no doubt about that. Early in the eighth century Ina, King of the West Saxons, endowed the church at Sarisbyrig with lands. The Danes captured Sarisbyrig from the Saxons, and later Alfred the Great drove out the Danes. Alfred, a military leader of genius, realized (as must have every other military leader before him) the supreme strategical importance of the place and ordered Leofric to preserve and strengthen the defences. In 960 King Edgar summoned a Parliament here which was attended by " all the nobles of the realm ". In 1003 Sweyn burnt and sacked Wilton and then proceeded to hand out the same fate to Sarisbyrig. Undoubtedly Sarisbyrig was a place of importance. But very little that is Saxon has been found at Old Sarum. Yet if Sarisbyrig was not Old Sarum, where was it? It has never been found and the whole of this area has been intensively surveyed and excavated. It is even more strange that it should not have been found than that so little that is Saxon should have been found at Old Sarum. It must be remembered, too, that Alfred found fortifications— obviously good ones—and gave instructions that they should be preserved and strengthened. The only place in the neighbourhood answering in the smallest degree to this description is Old Sarum. Personally I am convinced that Sarisbyrig is Old Sarum, and that for once the Saxons, in view of its evident strategical value, broke their rule, and lived in a hill-top town.

Be that as it may, there can be no doubt that the Normans took over the site, for Norman remains, from pottery to the remnants of the great walls that now crown the ancient Neolithic earthworks, have been found in profusion. In Norman times a great town grew up here. It was not only the seat of an earldom with a great castle, but it was also the seat of a bishop with a cathedral, and apart from this dual importance it was a populous place. It is the more astonishing, therefore, that it should have been deserted.

It is difficult now to imagine Old Sarum as once it must have been. Now we see just a great mound, and when we are within it shape and plan are lost, and we are in a ruin without form. Actually Old Sarum consists of two mighty earthworks, the one within the other, and the great mound is built up in three tiers. The top is an irregular oval of about thirty acres, and in the centre of it is a raised circular platform. The whole great earthwork was originally surrounded by a deep ditch (now broken and crossed by causeways) and the interior platform was also surrounded by a deep ditch with a high rampart on the inward bank. This interior platform was the site of the Norman castle. At the time when that castle was occupied it seems that the area between the two earthworks, the outer and the inner, was divided in two by two great banks running north and south. The eastern half was the outer bailey of the castle and was occupied mainly by the civil population, the western half

THE OLD MILL, AT BREAMORE

FORDING-
BRIDGE

was the ground of the bishop and the cathedral was situated at the northernmost end of it. Thus the cathedral stood on the broad level plateau just below the castle, and very close to it.

The cathedral was begun by Bishop Hermann about 1070. Hermann was an Alsatian, who had held a bishopric (that of Ramsbury) under the Saxon kings, but for some reason he did not lose his post under the Normans. Indeed, the Norman Conquest seems to have resulted in a good deal of favour being shown to him, for he was one of those who assisted at the consecration of Lanfranc and he was also present at the Council of London. Hermann died in 1078, before his cathedral was completed, and the work was continued and completed by his successor, Bishop Osmund. It was consecrated by Walkelin, Bishop of Winchester, in 1092. Five days after its consecration it was struck by lightning and partially destroyed. William of Malmesbury records this storm :

> In the fifth year [of William II's reign] a thunderstorm similar to that which in the previous year had devastated London, entirely destroyed the roof of the church tower and much injured the wall at Sarum, only five days after Osmund, the bishop of famous memory, had consecrated it.

Evidently the church was very badly destroyed, for the same chronicler, under the date 1119, tells us that Roger, who was Osmund's successor and who held the see from 1107 to 1139, " built anew the church of Sarum and adorned it in such a manner that it yields to none in England, but surpasses many, so that he had just cause to say ; Lord, I have loved the glory of Thy House ".

This Bishop Roger is one of the great men in English history. A Norman by birth he was a priest at Caen when he attracted the attention of Prince Henry Beauclerc (afterwards Henry I of England) who, when he ascended the throne, made him his Chancellor. In 1102 he gave him the Bishopric of Sarum, but Anselm, Archbishop of Canterbury, refused his consent for some reason that is not clear, and it was not until 1107 that he was consecrated. There was, I imagine, some jealousy between Anselm and Roger, the former recognizing a great man when he saw one, and fearing for his own position. However, in those days it was more than a little dangerous to cross a king, and in due course Roger triumphed and got his see. Shortly afterwards he was made Justiciar, and William of Malmesbury tells us that he had the whole governance of the kingdom. Undoubtedly he was the ruler of England when the King was away, and he had the charge of Duke Robert of Normandy, holding him prisoner " as a noble pilgrim " at Devizes and perhaps also at Sarum. On the death of Henry, Roger sided with Stephen. Stephen retained him as Justiciar and, indeed, declared that he would give him half the kingdom if he wished it. Roger had no need of such a gift—he already controlled the whole kingdom. His mistress was Matilda of Ramsbury, and she held the castle of Devizes. His son by her, also named Roger, was Chancellor of England. His nephew, Nigel, was Treasurer of England and also Bishop of Ely. His nephew, Alexander, was Bishop of Lincoln. He himself was Justiciar, and Bishop of Sarum, and lord of the castles of Sarum, Malmesbury, Sherborne. He had built all these castles and fortified them. His nephews had done the same in their dioceses, his son in his. It is little wonder that such success aroused the jealousy of the barons, and in 1137 he was accused of treason. Stephen demanded his presence and that of his son and nephews at Oxford, and they went there on June 24th, 1139. The very fact that they went, knowing well why they were required (for they must have known), suggests that Roger was innocent of treason. Stephen demanded the keys of their castles. They would not give them up, and were arrested. Nigel, however, escaped and fled to Matilda of Ramsbury at Devizes. Stephen marched against her and took his prisoners with him. When Matilda refused to surrender he starved the elder Roger, and let her know that he was doing so, and she surrendered. Roger's three castles fell to the keeping of the King. But there it ended. The Bishop of Winchester, the Papal Legate and the King's brother himself saw to it that he kept the castle at Sarum and his nephews those that went with their sees. Moreover, the King had to do penance for his treatment of them. If Roger's power was lessened he was far from defeated. But, in fact, the treatment he had received at the hands of Stephen proved too much and he died in December of the same year.

During Roger's tenancy of the see Sarum was a great and prosperous place. It all belonged to him, castle no less than cathedral. But when he died the castle passed out of the hands of the bishop, and from that moment trouble began. There was now a dual control in the hill town. And it was because of this dual control that the place was finally deserted.

Sarum is not, of course, the only town in Britain that has migrated bodily. There have been a number of cases of small towns being deserted and rebuilt a short distance away. For the most part such migrations have been caused by the encroaching sea—Winchelsea is a good example—but here there was nothing of that sort. All that was the matter was that the military held sway on the upper plateau, the clergy on the lower. There was not enough space within the encircling walls for the two to live in amity. The military soon began to bully the clergy, and life for the latter and their tenants was scarcely worth living. " After brawls they often fell at last to blows." The cathedral was too close to the castle, and there were frequent boundary disputes. Once, while the clergy were going in procession to the cathedral the military chose that moment for one of these boundary squabbles, and " the entertainment waxed hot ". Once the military shut the clergy out from the cathedral and from their homes and made them spend a cold winter night in the open. More than once they refused them entry to the cathedral to conduct services. So bad did it become that finally, Peter of Blois (using strangely modern idiom) exclaimed before the assembled clergy : " What has the House of the Lord to do with castles ? In God's name let us get out of here. Let us descend to the level. There, are rich fields and fertile valleys abounding in the fruits of the earth and watered by living streams."

And so, though after much hesitation, the move was made. And with the clergy went the townspeople. The military were left on their own. Soon Sarum was deserted. Soon it became Old Sarum.

But, deserted, it was yet to play a part in English history. It was to attain fame as a pocket-borough. In Leland's day there was a chapel still in use, though no one lived on the hill and the old town was but a few scattered ruins. In Pepys's day it was utterly deserted, even the chapel had fallen. " So all over the plain by the sight of the steeple, and to Salisbury by night. But before I come to the town I saw a great fortification, and there lit, and to it, and find it prodigious, so as to fright me to be in it alone at that time of night, it being dark. I understand since it to be that which is called Old Sarum." This deserted, ruined mound was allotted two seats in Parliament by Edward I, and these seats it held until the time of the Reform Bill. Presumably at the time that Edward granted the seats there were nine people holding land on the hill, even if they were not actually living there, for nine scattered plots of land, amounting in all to 23 acres, each conferred a vote. Later, however, all these plots came into the possession of the Lord of the Manor, who, in order to fulfil the regulations, used to grant leases to two people, who having registered their votes for the man put up by the Lord of the Manor, then relinquished their rights in the land until they were required for duty at the next election. It is said that the Lord of the Manor of Old Sarum, having had a tiff with the Prime Minister of the day, once threatened to send his negro servant to Parliament —and gained his point forthwith. Old Sarum was by no means the least comic of the many comic pocket-boroughs.

But now, standing on the hill—a huge crater now—there is nothing comic at all. The place is vast and grim and desolate. The massive ruined walls and the gravel paths and the carefully-sited staircases combine to drive home the sadness and desolation. That is so, even on a fine summer day.

Then the prospect from the top is magnificent. The Plain stretches far to the north, brightly coloured at the very foot of the hill and fading gradually to a soft grey, the dark clumps of fir and beech standing up clear and sharp in the foreground, mere black specks in the distance, serving to emphasize distance. The white chalk roads glisten in the sun, run like thin tapes over the distant hills by the hidden Vale of Pewsey. In September the broad bands of stubble are golden, the turnips a twinkling green, the Downs gentle. Southward Salisbury, the city of New Sarum, and but a mile and a half away, the great spire rising a hundred feet above the rampart on which you stand; the soft thickly wooded valleys, " the living streams " of Wylye and Nadder coming to join Avon, the broadened stream running away to the distant hills. Shut your eyes to the red roofs, and the factories and the railway sidings (even, if you can, to the spire) and you can realize just what poor persecuted Peter of Blois felt all those years ago.

But this evening as I wandered in the rain round the great earthwork—it is rather more than a mile round, just a little less than the boundary of Avebury—I could see nothing at all of a view. From the top I could not even see the great spire I knew was so near. Everything was blotted out by the steady downpour. Here was desolation indeed, grey and cold and damp.

I went down into Salisbury.

## CHAPTER IV

## SALISBURY

It is curious the hold certain places get on you. I am sure that it is possible to love a place with almost as deep an attachment as you feel for a person. It is a different sort of feeling, of course : different because places are less subject to change than persons, and so there is less risk involved in the attachment.

Attachment for a person is very often the result of an impression made at some particular moment, and never forgotten. In my own case this is often a first impression, and thereafter the attachment may or may not grow. But, no matter what may happen to the personal relationship, the impression remains, surviving all change, surviving even the loss of contact over many years.

It is the same with places. Because places do change, even as people change. But there is, as with people, that first impression or the impression made at some particular moment. As with people the attachment may or may not grow. Permanent residence may strengthen it to the point of intimacy or may diminish it, but the original impress remains. Nothing, in my experience, can kill that. It may be that you love a place (as often you love a person) because of the memory of some incident—even an imagination—that occurred at some particularly impressionable moment in the past. Absence keeps such a memory alive, may even strengthen it—absence, as some cynic once remarked, makes the heart grow fonder—for there is no risk of continuous presence. You do not realize actuality. I have such a fondness for Shrewsbury, because of a narrow lane on a blustery winter night ; for Monmouth, because of a smell on the old bridge one hot summer noon ; for Exeter, because of the crying of a little owl from the trees by the cathedral the night of a September full moon. But I do not know these towns. Their names bring back memories, vivid impressions, and the attachment is the stronger because I do not know them. To realize actuality you must visit and leave and return, visit and leave and return, many times.

I suppose that it will appear to many an affectation to speak of loving places as one loves people. It may appear the more affected in an avowed countryman. I love the country. I love wild country, mountains no less than marshes, pathless country. I prefer to spend a day on a marsh than a day in London. But it is merely morbid—if it is not an unhealthy perversion—to pretend, as some people do, that one would rather live in the wilderness, far from the paths of men. Byron, I know, professed to love nature more than man. But Byron had no desire to become a hermit. The solitary, the man who professes to love the wilderness so much more than the habitations of man that he forsakes them altogether, has met with disaster and is seeking consolation where complete consolation will never be found. Solitude is often preferable to society—always preferable to some society—but continuous solitude leads to insanity.

I am a countryman, and I love the country. I can spend a day, a week, in wild country—days without spending a minute in company other than my own—and not be lonely or bored, for I have an absorbing interest in any form of wild life. But I know that it is always the human that gives significance, that enhances the value—more often than not that gives beauty—to wild country. I have walked many miles of lonely road and I have learnt that the road is dearer, the memory of it more pressing, for the scent of cottage woodsmoke drifting across the hedgerow. I have slept out in the open many nights in all weathers and all sorts of country, and not been lonely or oppressed by the wildness, but I have learnt that the Gypsy fire makes the wildness dearer, the memory more pressing. I have looked at many a deep wood from some bare hillside, at many a lonely valley from mountain-side, and known that I was looking at beauty, but the woods and the valleys I remember are not those that were completely deserted, but rather those where a blue wisp rose from some hidden cottage chimney. Something personal, I am convinced, always attaches to the place we love. There must always be something that links it with man. It is that link I mean, when I speak of loving a place as one does a person. It is not only the stone and the brick and the slate, the macadam and the paving, but the human behind it all.

To return to a place you love is always impressive. It may be sad. Madame de Staël spoke of travel as " the saddest of all pleasures ". That is a generalization that can apply only to particular instances, as is the way with generalizations. There can be nothing sad about seeing a beautiful place for the first time (there may be regret that we have come too late, but that is a different matter), but there is always pleasure. There should, I think, always be more pleasure than pain in returning to a place you love. You may return alone where once you went in companionship : there will be sadness at the loss of company, the memory of loss—and that is sad—but there will also be the memories, the memories crowding one upon another, of that companionship and the joys it brought. Inevitably, there will be the sense of the passage of time, and all that that means, yet even that should not swamp the pleasure that was there. It may be that the return to a place loved means the meeting with ghosts. There are many people who shrink from that, many people who would always rather forget than remember. Yet even the meeting with ghosts—the ghosts of loved ones no longer with us—though sad should be stimulating. Yes, even the meeting again with the ghost that is ourselves (and that must happen wherever we return), though often unpleasing, must always be stimulating.

And so, coming again to Salisbury, I felt excitement rising within me. I do not know what it is that makes me love Salisbury. I have never lived in the town, but I have visited it often—so often that I have long since lost count—

and always I have this pleasurable excitement that I experienced the first time, now more than thirty years ago, an excitement that has grown with the years.

Salisbury has changed tremendously in recent years. It has grown, not only in size but in manner. In some indefinable way it has acquired a second being. No longer is it a cathedral city and a market-town. Both it is still, but now also it is modern and twentieth-century. So that there is still the warm personal Salisbury, and around it and cloaking it a crust that is quite impersonal, that might be anywhere, that has nothing more to do with Salisbury than the accident that it is there. It is a change large enough to have shattered any relationship between persons : it has left untouched my attachment for Salisbury.

Once there was a time, which I remember, when Old Sarum was separated from Salisbury. You walked downhill between hedgerows, and then quite suddenly you were in Salisbury and right into the town at a step. I am not suggesting that there was not a suburb on this side of the town, for there was, but it was a suburb that was part of the being of the town, as the squares of Kensington are a part of London. Now, you step from Old Sarum into a modern suburb.

Too little attention is paid to suburbs. They are, perhaps, the most important feature of modern England. Certainly, when the ordinary Englishman is abroad or at the wars, he does not think back, as many would have us believe, to green fields and quiet streams ; he does not think back, as some would have us believe, to red coats and the sound of the horn and the sight of hounds streaming away in pursuit of the fox ; he thinks back to a small neat house with everything in its right place. And that, too, is what the ordinary Englishman, living in digs in the middle of a town, dreams of —the day when he can afford a small neat house on the outskirts, with everything in its right place, and a well-mown lawn and Virginia creeper on the walls, and a nice girl to look after it and him. The size of the house will vary, of course, and the setting will vary : Streatham Vale, for some

and a very small lawn very well mown ; Purley for others,
and a larger house and a very well mown lawn. London
or Birmingham, Bristol or Manchester, Leeds or Liverpool,
Glasgow or Cardiff, it does not matter—essentially the picture
is the same. Except for the very rich (who are cosmopolitan
anyhow, and in these days almost certainly foreigners), except
for the very poor, maybe (though I believe that the very
poor dream the same dreams as the rest of us), except for
a few " intellectuals ", except for the freaks and the fortunate,
the suburban villa with everything in its right place is the
dream of the ordinary Englishman.

We pay too little attention to suburbs for another reason.
The suburban villa provides in every age a distinct architectural type. And this architectural type is always reviled.
The term used to describe this suburban architecture between
the wars was " Jerrybethan "—which speaks for itself. It
is a term of abuse, of scorn. People of taste, especially
" intellectuals ", shuddered and turned away when confronted
with the speculative builder's achievement between the wars.
The little house—the Tudor of the half-inch boards—that
lines the arteries out of the big cities was held up as the
supreme example of depravity in taste.

Yet millions of people lived in them happily. Millions
more dreamed of living in similar houses one day.

I cannot pretend that I like Jerrybethan. I admit that
I would much prefer the old approach to Salisbury from
Old Sarum. But I believe that the fierce, almost fanatical,
criticism of suburban architecture springs from ignorance of
the instincts and ideals it sets out to satisfy, and which, on
the whole, it has satisfied extremely well. The architecture
of the suburb is the true expression of the contemporary
vernacular. It has, I think, always been so. The Jerrybethan was the expression of the age between the wars. It
could not have occurred at any other time. In the same
way the slate roof, the ornamental tiles along the ridge, was
the expression of the 'nineties. It could not have occurred
at any other time. It did not occur at any other time.

We spend a lot of time looking at ancient buildings. We

know the various periods of church architecture—Norman, Gothic, and so on : we know certain periods of domestic architecture—Tudor, Queen Anne, Regency : we trace development by these styles, we set periods to time and achievement. But we ignore the architecture of the suburbs. And yet it is by this despised architecture that you may most clearly see the growth and development of a town. And in Salisbury you can see it all, all the gradual spread out from the old city in the centre.

Just out from the centre—on the edge of what was once the country—are the suburbs of the 'eighties and 'nineties. The houses are tall with a slate roof more frequently than a tiled one, but always there is a crest of ornamental tiles along the ridge ; the gables are steep with perforated barge-boards painted green (though I remember a temporary Salisbury fashion for red) ; the windows are sash ; the walls (when not covered with ivy) are of red and yellow bricks arranged in geometrical patterns, or of a greyish rough-cast ; there is a porch, its sides panelled with glass of different colours, standing at the head of a flight of steps ; there is usually a small round window set in the point of the gable. There are hundreds and hundreds of similar houses in London, Birmingham, Manchester, Bristol, Leeds, all over England. In the 'eighties and 'nineties they were the dream of the Englishman overseas or at the wars or in digs in the middle of the town. No doubt in the 'eighties and 'nineties they caused people of taste to shudder.

A little further out—and some twenty-five years later— the architecture has changed. The houses are more cheerful in colour—red instead of grey or yellow and red, a bright beef red ; the roofs are tiled, red tiles, with dormer windows. These Edwardian houses are less upright in shape, and altogether less grim in aspect, and the over-all redness is relieved by plenty of white paint ; white-painted woodwork round the windows, themselves divided by thick bars (painted white) into rectangular squares ; white-painted balconies ; a white-painted verandah instead of the porch. You rarely find ivy on the walls of these houses—instead a creeper.

145

There are hundreds of similar houses in London, Birmingham, Manchester, Bristol, Leeds, all over England. Before the first World War they were the dream of the Englishman overseas or at one of the little wars of Empire or in digs in the middle of the town or in the earlier suburb. No doubt in the years preceding the first World War they caused people of taste to shudder.

And after the first World War? Well, still the cheerful red (though now often only in roofs or chimney stacks), but the white paint has gone. Instead there is a natural-coloured oak. But the large gable has come back, in exaggerated form, so that in many instances you find it extending almost to the ground, forming the front of the house. Oak-beams— half-inch boards nailed to the wall—criss-cross the gable; there is a porch, but now it is shaped like a lych-gate; the windows are of metal, leaded into diamond panes. Crazy-paving runs to the front door. There are hundreds of similar houses in London, Birmingham, Manchester, Bristol, Leeds, all over England. In the second World War they were the dream of the Englishman overseas. Between the wars they were the dream of the Englishman overseas or at one of the small wars of Empire or in digs in the middle of the town or in one of the earlier suburbs. Between the wars they caused people of good taste to turn away with a shudder.

Obviously, there is something wrong here. Here in generation after generation is depravity, lack of taste : yet here in generation after generation is what ninety out of every hundred Englishmen want, and save and skimp to get. Suburban England is the background most of us know, in which most of us grew up, to which most of us retire, in which most of us die. Have we all got depraved taste ?

Taste apart, it is evident that suburbs have charm. The rich, the freak, the intellectual, the fortunate may deny it, but the fact remains—suburbs have charm. There is a suburban appeal. And how interesting and revealing suburbs are ! You can trace the modern history of a town through its suburbs ; the increase in population, prosperity and decay,

new industries, new amusements, all leave their traces on
suburbs rather than on the town's centre. So walking into
Salisbury, you can see, as you pass the various stages of the
city's development.

Salisbury is, of course, unique among cathedral cities.
It has not grown up higgledy-piggledy through Roman,
Saxon, Norman times. It was deliberately planned on
entirely new, and level, ground about 1220. It has, therefore, a much more regular plan than other ancient towns.
" Ancient " is a relative word in this case, for Salisbury is
the latest of all the towns of southern England. Wholly
ecclesiastical in origin, it has grown, as is fitting, more or
less to the plan laid down by Bishop Poore.

Wholly ecclesiastical in origin : you cannot get away
from the cathedral in Salisbury. You cannot get away from
the past—even though the past is not quite so insistent as
it is in Winchester, for example. There is Old Sarum,
looming there but a short distance away, an ever-present
reminder of the prehistoric past : there is the great plain,
unseen from the city's centre, yet always present ; there is
always the knowledge that Stonehenge and its mystery are
close at hand. But it would be foolish in the extreme to
imagine Salisbury a dead place. It is a very busy market
town. There is a constant and very healthy bustle of life in
the market place and around the old Poultry Cross. The
shops are not merely local shops : they have no lack of
custom from the residents, no lack of custom from strangers
of whom there is a ceaseless stream, but also they serve a
wide area around, many a lonely village of the plain. Much
of this life has nothing whatever to do with the cathedral.
But it is the cathedral and the rivers that dominate Salisbury.
They are the abiding, the insistent, presences.

Five rivers meet at Salisbury—Avon, Wylye, Ebble,
Nadder and Bourne—and it was the rivers that brought
Salisbury down from the hill, that gave it life. It is proper
that one should always be conscious of them. It is the
rivers, too, that make the setting of the cathedral the most
pleasing, if not actually the most beautiful, in England.

When first the town moved down from the hills there was a village here. Fisherton village, now swallowed up, and remembered only by the bridge, from which, with the hubbub of traffic all around, you may see fat trout lying in the stream, from which small boys with string and a pin sometimes succeed in taking a fish that has defeated more serious anglers. Once just Fisherton village by the river—now Salisbury out to Bemerton, to Wilton really. But the rivers have not lost their identity. They remain a network of streams, confusing to follow, but always alluring. Always they lead you far out of the town, and always the lovely spire beckons you back. Always the spire.

There can be no doubt what Constable thought of the situation of Salisbury Cathedral. Hawthorne, when he came to Salisbury, thought the site finer than that of any other cathedral, and he was something of an expert in cathedrals. On this point there must inevitably be divergence of opinion. Cathedrals are, in any case, difficult to compare. So far as cathedral towns are concerned I think it must be a moot point as to which is the most perfect, Salisbury or Hereford. Personally, I think that Hereford must have the palm. For I believe that a cathedral town to be perfect must not be too large. It should be snug and free from smoke. It should not be industrial at all, not the centre of a mining or manufacturing area. It should be the county town and the centre of an agricultural area, and preferably a picturesque area. Hereford fulfils all the requirements : Salisbury does not. But there can be little or no divergence of opinion as to the satisfaction afforded by Salisbury Close, a beautiful sanctuary apart from yet close to the bustling centre of a busy market town. Wells has something of the same atmosphere, but with the difference that Wells is a small sleepy little town : Exeter has the nearness but not the aloofness : Winchester dominates. Salisbury, set in that wide Close, is supreme and superb.

But the cathedral itself is not to be known easily. By some it is never known. Henry James, another expert on cathedrals and one whose appreciation was more discriminating than that of many natives, was never won by Salisbury. Wells was always his favourite among English cathedrals. Hudson, another foreigner (though we are apt to forget that) was disappointed when first he visited Salisbury. He thought it appeared too new. He grew to love it in the end, but for long he thought it too flawless and too cold. Another who was disappointed was the American historian, Motley, author of *The Rise of the Dutch Republic*, but for another reason. He wrote in a letter to a friend:

This was the first specimen of the English Gothic I was to see, and as I walked thither my head was full of the Continental Gothic, which as yet was all I knew. I thought of the cathedrals of Cologne, Vienna, of Rouen, of strange unfinished, unfinishable buildings, built according to no plan, or rather according to a dozen different ones, and rising helter-skelter from the midst of a multitude of old, sharp-gabled, red-tiled, ten-storey houses, all looking as if built in the time of the Crusaders. The idea of a Gothic cathedral was associated in my mind with hundreds of tumble-down hovels, booths and shops, mixed grotesquely here and there with a magnificent palace of half a dozen centuries, so that on the whole, when I came to look on Salisbury Cathedral, I was most ridiculously half-disappointed.

Influenced by the associations I have mentioned, I thought the whole scene at first too tidy, too notable, too house-wifish; but, as I said before, this was only my own dulness; on second thoughts I acknowledged to myself that filth and poverty and ugliness were not necessarily concomitants of a cathedral, and I confessed that I had rarely seen a more lovely picture than this same church presents. The scene is so softly and sweetly English. The stately and graceful cathedral with its green and smooth-shaven lawn in front, the surrounding elm trees in their magnificent massive foliage; the tidy cottages half covered with honeysuckles and rose-bushes, the hawthorn hedges, and the green meadows with their sleek cattle (to say nothing of the macadamised turnpike and the new hotel) altogether make up a scene purely and exclusively English, and, perhaps, after all, as pleasing a one as you can find anywhere.

It is really the same complaint each time, each time the same fault is found—that the place looks too new. In 1220 it was started, and that is a long time ago. But it is true that Salisbury does not give an impression of great age. Of course, it is not as old as many cathedrals—as Canterbury or Winchester or Durham or Exeter or many more—but it is old, and yet looks always quite new. It is for that reason that it does not always impress at first sight—too new, too flawless. Salisbury is like a beautiful woman just out of a beauty parlour. And, of course, that is what Salisbury is—feminine. Winchester is altogether masculine, rugged and personal. Salisbury is delicate and cool and impersonal. But Salisbury grows on you, improves all the while on acquaintance—which is more than can be said for most women.

Of course, the present cathedral is not very much like the one that Bishop Poore started—at least so far as the interior is concerned. The great restorer, Wyatt, was employed here. His crimes are numberless, and none worse than those committed in this building. He, may he be forgiven in due course, opened up " vistas " (they were as fashionable as long skirts are now) and he destroyed almost all the stained glass. Nor was that all. He was followed by Scott in the middle of the last century. And Scott left the interior " varnished marble and quite bepainted and bedizened ".

But the exterior, by some miracle, escaped the attention of the restorers. What you see now is pretty well the church of the mid-fourteenth century. And you see it in surroundings that are the most gently beautiful of any English cathedral. I do not think there can be any doubt about that. That wide green Close is really beautiful, and the architecture around it is an epitome of the best English house design at the best periods.

But there can be no doubt that at first the very perfection

THE MILL AT
BICKTON

NEAR IBSLEY

of the exterior, the unity of it all, does seem strange—and even a little displeasing—when you are used to the rich variety of, say, Exeter or the rugged bulk of Winchester. Most great churches grow with the ages, and you can trace their development and their enrichment, their ancestry, in the stones, memorials to those who have laboured on them through the ages. Not so with Salisbury : Salisbury is a single scheme, most beautifully worked out. It is all one period—Early English. More than that : this is the only cathedral in England that can be seen, realized, the whole of it, at the first glance, and from many angles. I have heard it said that it looks like a model, a gigantic model placed on a green carpet, a model that might be lifted up and carried away by some huge power. There is a little truth in that statement. It does look a bit tidy. Some old churches, most old cathedrals, look as if they had grown from their bases, like a tree firmly rooted. There is nothing like that about Salisbury. The outlines of its base are far too clean and sharply defined. I have always thought that a few gravestones in the Close would give the suggestion of a more gradual approach, a reaching forth to the soil, like the tendrils from the roots of a tree. But there are no gravestones. The Close is level hard-mown green, as smooth as a billiard table. But once the Close was a burial ground, though you would never guess that normally just by looking at it. I found it out in 1947, by accident, in the heat wave.

I had walked some thirty miles the previous day, and slept at the Crown, because I was, after that long walk in great heat, in very urgent need of a hot bath. In the morning I wandered round the town and then made my way to the Close, and sat down on the grass with my back to the low wall. I was looking across at the cathedral. And suddenly I saw that there were patches on the grass—oblong patches, a deeper brown than the parched grass. They looked like pieces of matting laid out to dry, and for a moment I thought that they were cleaning the interior and that that was what had happened, that stretches of coconut matting had been brought out on to the grass to be cleaned. And then I realized that they were low-lying graves. It is more than one hundred years since anyone was buried in Salisbury Close. More than one hundred years ago the headstones of the graves were removed and the mounds of the graves levelled. The graves themselves were left undisturbed. It was thought that they would lie there undisturbed and undetected under the green sward. Here they were showing. Here, before my eyes, was proof of the truth of the saying that you cannot keep a good man down.

In any case what does it matter if it does look a little like a model of what a cathedral should be, a little too perfect? You can see it all at a glance, and that is the great thing. And how wonderful it is! Rising vast and shapely, a lofty pile of warm-hued greyish stone, tinged green with lichen, tier upon tier of it to the slender magnificence of the central tower, and poised above all, exquisite, the tallest, the loveliest spire in England. No, in the world. Nowhere in the world, I swear, is there greater beauty than this spire. There is no shyness about it. It gives all of itself, all its beauty, at once without reservation. And you come again and again and again to drink of it. Miles away you see it, miles in every direction, and every time you must get nearer, to have just one more look.

So far as I am concerned I have learned to love this cathedral by walking away from it. Every time the spire has caught my eye and beckoned me back, and I have responded to its silent appeal. You do not seem able to leave it, to lose sight of it, at least within the compass of a normal walk. Nor, to be frank, is there the desire to do so. It is so perfectly a part of its surroundings, whether you see it from Old Sarum, or from the Plain, or from the distant Downs, or from the water-meadows. But it is especially attractive from the bridge at the beginning of the way to Harnham. It was here that Constable had that revelation of it beneath a great rainbow—Hudson also saw it so, and from this spot too—but I have not been so fortunate. I have seen it under many atmospheric conditions—Salisbury lies in a hollow and the atmosphere is always changing—but that crowning glory has so far been denied me. However, even in settled weather, as in the long dry spell of 1921 or in the heat wave of 1947, there are constant changes of light and each one works a miracle. In unsettled weather, there is a wealth of such changes, so that now the spire looks black, and now white and shining like a sword against the dark rainclouds. From this bridge you get, of course, the picture-postcard view. It is so hackneyed that you would think it would be dull. But the postcards have not captured it. No painter, not even Constable, and no photographer, not even Kerr, has ever done it justice, let alone captured it. You cannot capture a spirit on paper.

I feel rather differently about the interior. I do not much care for it. Wyatt and Scott are to blame. There is no denying the magnificence of the vista from the west door, enhanced by that surprisingly beautiful screen. I can stand at the west door and look and look and be satisfied. But for the rest : grey Chilmark stone and varnished Purbeck. It is too light, too cool—frigid almost—for my taste. The contrast with the warm stone without is startling, so startling that it almost repels. The stone of the interior glistens in broad daylight. This is not, of course, the fault of the builders. They never dreamed that it would ever look like this. They arranged for colour and warm-stained glass. Then, indeed, it must have been as lovely inside as out. But Wyatt took the glass away. Normally time is the best colourist of all. In Salisbury Cathedral time has stood still. The workmanship is magnificent, but it was not meant to be seen in this light. It is all a little too thoroughly garnished and polished. And the choir—the work of that man Wyatt again—beggars description. You have got to see it to realize the full polychromatic horror of its painting and encaustic tiles, not to mention a full range of Scott fittings. It is an unhappy spectacle. There is still a notable series of old tombs, it is true—they escaped the attentions of Wyatt and Scott—but there is too little of mystery, too little of mysticism, too little, to be frank, of decay.

Perhaps it does not matter. Who visits cathedrals now? A small group of residents, a few inquisitive tourists, a few lovers of beauty. As someone once said, "What are they but the palaces of long-forgotten kings"? But I think it does matter. I think it matters terribly. Think what went to the making of them—the patience, the industry, the harsh discipline, the love of beauty, the sense of personal kinship with God. Towers and pillars, planning and painting, glass and woodwork, all were inspired by something that is missing from England to-day. Socialism is no substitute. The five-day week, and women working in the factories to make up the work the men will no longer do, is no substitute. What men faced in hard work and austerity for the love of God they will not face for the exhortations of a politician. It is something vital that has gone. But it will come back one day.

The wonderful thing about cathedrals—the lesson they have for all of us—is their patience. They were built for and dedicated to something greater and more permanent than fashions in architecture or personal taste. They know—as their builders knew—that truth is their foundation, truth and beauty. And so they can wait for ever.

And looking at Salisbury Cathedral you must have patience too. Patience with the interior. You must wait until twilight. That is the time to see the interior. Twilight brings a tender compensation, a suggestive concealment. Seen in the half-light, transepts and recesses wrapped in growing shadow, candles on the distant altar, the newness goes and the chill impersonality. In their stead comes awe. The building is haunted then with old prayer and liturgy. Stand then and look at the chantry monument of Bishop Giles de Bridport. It is one of the earliest of its kind, a most beautiful specimen of Geometrical Gothic, impressive even in daylight. But in the dim light of dying day, it seems to spring to life, and you are back in the thirteenth century. Architectural detail ceases to matter. Critics, specialists, writers, sightseers, all the complaints and worries and deadening regulations of the modern world, all are set aside. Twilight harmonizes and spiritualizes. Now, truly, is this the House of God, and here is the underlying kinship, the commerce with the unseen, the embrace of prayer.

But there is much else in Salisbury besides the cathedral. The place is not wholly dependent upon the cathedral for its attraction. It is quite true that wherever you go in Salisbury the cathedral seems to follow you ; but it is equally true that you lose sight of the building itself and so you can forget it easily enough. Quite apart from the cathedral a good deal of Salisbury is as attractive as its surroundings. There are still many fine old buildings ; there is still Lord Montacute's lovely fourteenth-century Poultry Cross (it has, by the way, nothing whatever to do with poultry, and never had) ; there are still some lovely old houses (the best are those round the Close and that by Crane Bridge) ; there are still some old inns. It is still possible in Salisbury to pause every few yards to admire something both old and beautiful. And of course, there is much more that has now been hidden behind brick or plaster—some of the interiors are magnificent. Yes, there is still much remaining. But much has been pulled down. I cannot walk round Salisbury without fear in my heart. I cannot go to Salisbury now without the fear that some building that I particularly liked will have disappeared. The modern idea of "improvement" is to destroy. "Progress" is symbolized by the bull-dozer.

However, there are still old inns of charming frontage, still cafés in medieval houses, where you can take your tea in beamed and wainscoted rooms. It is better to do so in the winter months if you want to see anything. There is bustle in Salisbury always, but in the summer the bustle is such that peace almost disappears. Coach after coach deposits its trippers for an hour or so, and the streets are crowded with men and women, anxious not to see the sights (though the cathedral does attract a few) but to squeeze in a meal or a drink. Most of them are on their way to the coast or to Stonehenge, but there will also be a few Americans seriously " doing " the town. Outside the tourist season the

bustle is a country bustle. Once the great market square was
the commercial centre of a region. Here you got the feel
of a busy agricultural community. It was a grand market,
noisy and virile and flourishing, and you would see there
the true country folk from the Plain and the hills of Dorset
and the wooded valleys running south to the sea, small
farmers and their wives, drovers and shepherds, all making
of their business a day's holiday. Then the inns did a
roaring trade; then the farmers' ordinaries were extraordinary. And all about you would be the rich voices of
Wessex, all of a family but with minute differences between
the tongues of Wiltshire and Dorset and Hampshire, minute
differences even between the tongues of this Plain village
and that. Now, the market is but a shadow of its old self.
Men still stand about the old square, there is still some half-
hearted business. But this is no longer a market in the true
sense. A market is free, and now we are controlled. Prices
are controlled, there are endless regulations for this and that,
there are inspectors to see that those regulations are observed,
to enforce them if necessary. They are broken, of course,
but in a furtive manner. The old freedom, the old rather
boisterous friendliness, so characteristic of the English market
at its best, has gone. Regulation and control, the distant
but ever-present hand of bureaucracy, as cold as a dead cod;
the chilling voice of Whitehall; the forms and the files;
these things have killed the spirit of the markets of England,
in many cases have killed the markets themselves.

You still hear the rich voices, of course. But they, too,
are going. Individuality is dying fast in Britain. In the
mountains of Wales, in the Highlands of Scotland, in very
remote villages and hamlets far from the track of the tourist,
in such places you still find individual speech; you may
even find a " character " or two. But elsewhere speech is
becoming standardized rapidly and characters have already
disappeared. (Winston Churchill's great hold on the imagination of the British people is due not to his genius—the
British distrust and dislike genius as such—but to the fact
that in an age that is without character in its people he is a

character.) In part; the service of the B.B.C. from London is to blame ; the carefully impersonal voices of the announcers —especially those reading the news—have been taken as the standard for correct speech ; but more the blame must rest on the modern school-teacher. Everything is done in these days to persuade country children that a white-collar future is the only future, and with the white collar goes the standard speech. It is a pity.

Other things are going. In the old market there used to be a number of bookstalls. Cathedral cities are usually good places for second-hand books, and Salisbury is no exception. It has, in fact, one of the best second-hand bookshops in the country. A second-hand bookshop will always lure me over the street wherever I may be—I have spent far too much money in this shop hard by the cathedral—but much more alluring are the stalls of books in the open air. Tucked away in the midst of meat and poultry and drapery and old china and sweets, they had an attraction for me that could not be resisted. I can never see one of these stalls without remembering Johnson's penance in the market-place at Uttoxeter, because he had on one occasion refused to attend his father's stall there. I never visit a market-place that has no bookstall without feeling horribly deflated. It is alto-gether a charming custom this, of bringing books into the market-place. But it is a custom that is dying rapidly. The day of the market bookstall has not yet gone completely, but whereas there used to be three or four stalls in Salisbury square, the last time I was there one only remained, and that one no longer quite the same.

In olden days, pre-1914 that is, countrymen loved these stalls. They would pore over the old volumes and handle many before they would pay their sixpence or their threepence and take away one battered volume to be read and re-read and treasured for years to come. I knew one old man who had bought one book a week for more than fifty years, and read them all, and he was better educated than many a man I have known with the best education that money could buy. Times were different then. There were long winter evenings to pass away. And so the bookstall with its row of eighteenth-century classics—Beattie, Collins, Gray, Thomson, Pope, Ossian—its Palgraves and Wordsworths and Tennysons—was much patronized. But now there are other attractions, the winter evenings are no longer there to be filled by one's own initiative. The cinema and the radio are everywhere for the asking. Reading has become the last refuge of the bored—even the newspapers have become mere series of headlines, potted information for paste minds. There was a brief revival after the first World War in the second-hand book trade, because there was a dearth of new publications for a time. There was a stronger revival during the second World War for the same reason and also because the black-out prevented many people from going out to the cinema. But already it is dying. Any dealer will tell you that to-day half his stock so far as selling value is concerned is so much waste paper. The paper back—a most welcome return to sanity—has also played its part in the virtual extinction of the market bookstall. It is not the young that you will see at a market bookstall to-day. The customers will all be elderly, and for the most part they still buy the classics and the poetry. The young do not read to-day for pleasure, so it seems to me (I am generalizing, of course) and certainly not for education. They read to be thrilled or to pass the boredom of a railway journey or a bus ride or a meal in a canteen.

I miss the market-place bookstalls in Salisbury, but the second-hand shop still flourishes—it does not have much that is very cheap unfortunately—and serves to heighten the literary atmosphere of the city. There is, of course, no actual atmosphere at all. Nothing is done in Salisbury to remind you that the city has any literary connections at all. But if you read you cannot but be aware all the time as you walk around. I find this even more so in Alton, where I am always conscious of the presence in some indefinable manner of Gilbert White and old Curtis, of Jane Austen and Mrs. Gaskell, of Charles Kingsley and Mary Mitford, but especially of White and Jane Austen. And so it is with Salisbury. Here Fielding lived and here he wrote the major part of *Tom Jones*. The original of Thwackum in that great work was one Hele, then headmaster of the Grammar School, where Joseph Addison was educated. But it is not of Addison that I think of when I am in Salisbury—I always have to think very hard to remember that he had any connection with these parts at all—it is not even of Fielding and *Tom Jones* that I think, though in fact *Tom Jones* is one of my favourite books. I think of Anthony Trollope.

I cannot enter the Close without seeing old Mr. Harding, venerable and silver-haired, tottering across the green to his last service in the cathedral. I cannot pass the Deanery without seeing the tall figure, so very dignified, and the scholarly face of Dr. Arabin. I cannot pass the Palace gates without seeing Mr. Crawley, weak and tired after his twenty mile walk from Hogglestock Vicarage, poor Mr. Crawley, half-starved and threadbare, but proud and erect, going to that immortal interview with the bishop and Mrs. Proudie. I see every time I am at that narrow gateway to the Close the carriages of the Bishop and Archdeacon Grantley. The delicate question of precedence; Griselda Grantley, her Viscount safe in the bag, imperturbable with thoughts for nothing but her trousseau; Mrs. Proudie, furious that Archdeacons must be noticed, but forced to make the courteous gesture; her husband, small and henpecked, by her side; the Archdeacon, so well-bred and so punctilious, as furious as Mrs. Proudie that he must doff his hat; the respective coachmen, pretending to take the sides of their employers, their faces almost as eloquent as those of the Archdeacon and the Bishop's wife, though I suspect that they would take a glass together in one of the old inns in the evening and speak together in a friendly and agreeable manner about the foolishness of the clergy. All through Salisbury I come upon the characters of Trollope. So real are they in the books that as I read I feel I know them and their faces are before me. And here the quiet lawns and the narrow thoroughfares are peopled with shadowy figures that are really very far from shadows.

And the other thing that I like so much about Salisbury is the water. It is difficult in Salisbury to be away from the sound of water. There are endless little runnels all over the place and there are also, of course, the five rivers. And perhaps the most delightful feature of the city is that you may stand in the very heart of the traffic and watch the trout lying in the clear shallows beneath Fisherton Bridge. And the shallows are clear. This is really very surprising. One would expect—at least that is my experience of town streams— all sorts of things in those shallows ; dead cats, old shoes, discarded motor tyres, tin cans, orange peel. I do not know if you have ever looked into the Wey at the bottom of Guildford High Street ? That is a normal town stream for England. Here it is different. The streams are clear and gentle and but moderately swift (it is difficult to believe that many times in the past flood waters from Wylye and Avon and Nadder have put three feet of water on the cathedral nave) and they chatter as they run. As you come out on to the water-meadows—the streams still a network, so that it is quite impossible to tell which river you are following, all identity has been lost and it is mere waste of time trying to identify the stream by which you walk—the rushes and the little bridges and the stepping stones make it difficult to believe that you are but a few yards from a busy city. There is noise, of course ; it is impossible to move anywhere in southern England nowadays without the sound of an aeroplane overhead at some time in the day and at Salisbury there is also the sound of the railway—it is a big and busy station and the engines seem to do rather more puffing because of it, as though they were conscious that this place was something out of the ordinary—and of motor traffic too. But there is also the sound of babbling water, and the quacking of ducks and sometimes, not infrequently, the majestic airborne passage of swans from one stretch of water to another.

I have said that you cannot identify the various streams here. But there can be no doubt that the presiding stream is the Nadder. In fact, when you come to view the five

Streams one after another, you can have little doubt that it is not a question of four of them joining the Avon at Salisbury, but rather that four of them join the Nadder at Salisbury. You get that impression just from looking at their waters. Below Salisbury—" the Pan or Receyver of most part of the water of Wyleshire ", as Leland put it—all five combine to make a noble stream, but at Salisbury there can be no doubt which is the most important, for all that custom and the geography books give precedence to the Avon. And geology shows that the impression gained from the eyes is right. The Nadder is the original stream, and its former course continued eastwards from Salisbury. The Avon was its tributary and its outlet was the great Solent river of prehistoric times. Later on when the water levels fell, the eastern part became the Test, and the remainder found a new outlet by flowing southward to Christchurch. But, still, the Nadder looks the part and dwarfs the others, if not in actual size at least in personality. In length it cannot compare with the Wylye or the Avon above Salisbury or the Bourne, which though a singularly undistinguished stream, is a very long one. Only the Ebble is inferior in length. But the volume of water coming down is another matter. The Nadder runs with purpose and determination, a full-blown river all the way. The Wylye has its source at the furthest limit of the chalk downs only one mile from Stourhead, the source of yet another river that comes into the Avon at Christchurch, and that is a long way indeed. But the Wylye at its beginnings is a winterbourne, that characteristic watercourse of the chalk, and it is a long way before it takes on the semblance of a river.

No, the Nadder is the foremost stream of the five, and a fine and richly decorated river too. How the name is derived, I do not know. Avon is easy—the ancient British, the modern Welsh, *afon*, which means simply a river : Bourne is easy in a like manner. But Nadder and Wylye and Ebble are not easy. I find it difficult to accept Camden's rather childish suggestion that the name was given to the stream because " it creepeth with crooked windings like an adder ".

I find it equally difficult to accept Spenser's suggestion for the Wylye

> Wiley bourn with passage slye
> That of his wyliness his name doth take.

These are just very old country folk-names, and their meanings are lost in antiquity. But I think it safe to say that not one of the three—Nadder, Wylye, Ebble—is English in origin. Wylye at least is not. This surely is an English corruption of the Welsh word Gwili. And has not this Wiltshire river an equally lovely sister tumbling temperamentally through the steep wooded valleys of Carmarthen?

The Nadder flows past Bemerton, now a suburb of Salisbury, and past the parsonage garden that George Herbert once loved so dearly and where he wrote the poetry and music that went so well with his quiet saintliness. Twice a week the poet would walk into Salisbury over the water-meadows, walking within sound of the music of running water all the way to hear the service music at the end. It is not often that you will find this practical association with music in our English poets, though almost all of them pay lip-service to it. Beyond question it is this practical association that gives a human touch to the Anglican Herbert as it does also to the Puritan Milton.

Herbert, of course, lived at the time when English church music was at its best. I suppose that it is absurd to compare the choral and instrumental renderings of to-day with those with which Herbert was familiar. Our resources are greater and the style is much more ornate. But it is as well to remember, when thinking of Herbert, that he was familiar with the compositions of Byrd and Gibbons and Tallis, and that they did for the Anglican service very much what Carissimi and Palestrina did for the Italian. Greater resources we may have, a more ornate style, but there cannot be the slightest doubt that there has been written little church music so pure and so dignified since Herbert's day.

One of the branches of the Nadder comes down from Fonthill, where it has been expanded into lakes and embellished with William Beckford's architectural extravaganzas, and towards its end it flows past the garden front of Wilton House, where with her " owne faire hands " Queen Elizabeth gave Sir Philip Sidney a lock of her hair. And in a few yards under a perfect Palladian bridge amid the formality of an Italian garden the Wylye joins it to form a big stretch of water reflecting great cedars.

I had to go out to Wilton, though strictly speaking it was not part of my walk (but then I had not kept very strictly to that all the way) because I have good friends there and in the immediate neighbourhood. And, on a more materialistic plane, I knew that all of them would be good for a free meal and they would not all be out. I walked the Bemerton way, because I find that two miles of broad, almost straight, high-way rather dull. Wilton is but a shadow of its former self. You feel tempted to say that it is shrinking, but in fact it is doing just the reverse. Its population is increasing and it is itself spreading. But once it was a great place with almost a nation-wide fame. Now it is but a little town on the very outskirts of Salisbury and shortly it will be in Salisbury, and just another suburb. They still make carpets here—and I hope that they always will, for Wilton was the first place in England to embark on this trade. Wilton made the first carpet ever woven in England. But as early as that one gets an insight into the throat-cutting habits of big business. In 1740, a Mr. Moody, a Welshman (there are still Welsh-speaking people in Wilton), was granted a patent for the exclusive right of making carpets of a certain kind in Great Britain, and he founded his factory at Wilton. But certain cunning persons in Kidderminster—their names are known and sound very un-English—obtained somehow (could it have been bribery ?) an insight into the process, so clear an insight that they were able to imitate it without breaking the letter of the law. Hence Kidderminster carpets at the expense of Wilton. But Wilton carpet has gained a reputation and this single factory still bravely withstands the pressing tide of modern standard-ization. I hope it always will. The town authorities of Wilton would be foolish to allow it to die in any case—there is more value in tradition than modern education and Socialist creed will admit.

The rest of the glories—all save one—have gone. Less than one hundred years ago the Assize occasionally sat at Wilton—and, as might be expected, it returned two members to Parliament until the Reform Bill—but now there is only Wilton House of all the glories of the past. Historically that past goes back a long way. It was here that the great struggle between the Kingdom of Wessex and the Kingdom of Mercia for supremacy in all England was finally decided by the victory of Egbert of Wessex in 823. Here Alfred fought the Danes, one of many rather indecisive skirmishes. And here the Danes under Sweyn utterly routed a Saxon Army and burnt Wilton to the ground. The Normans built it up again, and it was one of the first royal towns. Queen Maud, during the civil wars with Stephen, held her court here.

> The King Stephen a castle then began
> At Wilton, where Kyng David with power,
> And Erle Robert of Gloucester that was there,
> Him drove away out of that place full clere,
> And bet it downe to the ground full nere.

So, evidently, it was destroyed again. But destruction in those days was easily remedied. There was plenty of timber, and labour was easy enough to secure if you had armed forces to back your desires and cheap enough to employ. Wilton rose once again, and flourished until Bishop Bingham built his bridge at Salisbury. That bridge did more than all the armies and all the burning had done. It shut off Wilton from the western highway. If it did not destroy the place, it mummified it. Leland says that Wilton had twelve churches, and Colt Hoare claimed to have found the sites of them all. Myself, I find it difficult to believe that there were ever twelve churches in Wilton—I cannot see what need there would have been for them or where they could have been built—but if there were, in fact, twelve churches, then no more need be said of the importance of Wilton in the past. It must, indeed, have been a flourishing town.

Wilton church was built in 1844. It is an astonishing

edifice. It has absolutely nothing about it, save its situation, that is Wiltshire or even English. It is purely exotic. It is said to be in the Lombardic style—whatever that may mean precisely—but it does not seem to me to be wholly an Italian building. There is much that is pure Byzantine rather than Lombardic about it. It was designed by T. H. Wyatt, a younger relative of the man who ruined the cathedral at Salisbury, and it is, I understand, regarded by those who should know as a masterpiece of its kind. It may well be ; but I do not like it at all. The interior, I admit, is gorgeous. It should certainly be visited. It adds variety to a walk. But, more than that, it should be visited because, when you come out, you will appreciate the more the quiet beauty of the little Wiltshire houses and the absolute " rightness " of their traditional architecture.

Wilton House is another matter. It stands on the site of the great Benedictine Nunnery, which was second in importance (and antiquity) only to that of Amesbury. Many miracles were accomplished here—as is fitting in a great nunnery— and, as is also fitting, the breath of scandal did not pass it by. The ladies of Wilton were in their day (as were all the ladies of every other nunnery in the country that I have ever heard about), no better than they should have been, and all the more popular for that. It was this reputation that Henry VIII used to his advantage. Just before the dissolution Anne Boleyn— herself, perhaps, open to persuasion at times—wished to have a friend of hers installed as abbess. Henry VIII, who at that time was unable to deny the dark beauty from Wales anything but who, being in great need of money, had already decided on dissolution, put her off by saying, " I wolde not for all the golde in the world clog your conscience nor mine to make her a ruler of a house which is of so ungodly a demeanour ". This, from Henry, who would do anything for gold as readily as he would do anything for lust, is rich indeed, and the more so as it seems unlikely in the extreme that any friend of Anne Boleyn's would be easily shocked. In any case in 1535 Legh visited the house and four years later Wilton was surrendered. The abbess, who was one of the four who were peeresses of

England, received one hundred pounds and retired to Fovant, and the nunnery and the lands attached to it were granted by the King to Sir William Herbert, first Earl of Pembroke.

Herbert, a remarkable man who by "making good use of his opportunities during this eventful period managed to secure continued accession of power and wealth", pulled down all the monastic buildings including the church except one block of storehouses. Herbert then set about building a new house, using the stones of the old. Little, however, remains except the central block and this has been much altered. The porch of this is attributed to Holbein and is now a summer house, situated at the end of a magnificent avenue. Actually very little remained very long at Wilton. During the reign of Charles I the house was largely rebuilt by Solomon de Caus, and it was at this time that most of the gardens were laid out. Later, after a fire, it was restored by Webb, the son-in-law and assistant of Inigo Jones. For long the work was attributed to Inigo Jones himself. So were many other buildings up and down the country. But it would seem now that only the Banqueting House in Whitehall and the Queen's House at Greenwich can be regarded as authentic examples of his genius. Coleshill in Berkshire, which was for long regarded as his masterpiece, is now known to be the work of Sir Roger Pratt, one of his school. And there seems to be no doubt that the drawings for the proposed Palace of Whitehall were, like Wilton House, the work of Webb. For all that, it is Inigo Jones who is important. He founded the school, his stamp is indelibly set upon British architecture, he inspired the Webbs and the Pratts. But for him there would have been no Palladian glory in the eighteenth century. He may have had little or nothing to do with Wilton House, but without him there would have been no Wilton House as we know it to-day, "Gothicized" though it has been by Wyatt, altered as it has been again and again.

The gardens at Wilton owe much to de Caus. He it was who designed a terrace "for the more advantage of beholding those platts". De Caus was working at Wilton during the Civil War and must have been left quite undisturbed by the

THE AVON AT
RINGWOOD

THE AVON AT
SOPLEY

conflict. He must have had peace to get through so huge a project as this. And the garden that he laid out here was the first of those astonishingly elaborate gardens that became so popular after the Restoration. He set the fashion, but the description which he published of his garden at Wilton shows a comparatively simple design. There was a broad gravel path bisecting a huge level rectangle and passing through three equal divisions. The first of these was a knot garden, and this was subdivided by many smaller paths running at right angles each bordered by elaborate hedges of dwarf box. The second was symmetrically planted with trees in the style of a French *quinconce*. In the centre of each division was a circular open space, which contained a statue, and on the outer side of each grove was a covered alley ending in a circular pool. The third was a central walk, which widened out into an oval containing a statue ; beyond this was a wide belt of turf and beyond that a gravel path which followed the line of the central oval. Along the edge of the turf were lines of clipped trees—probably yews—while the central walk itself was finished with an arcaded loggia. Across the end of the rectangle ran a raised terrace with a balustrade on either side, hiding an orchard which lay beyond the main garden. This third division was the only one that was not so divided up that all sense of space and dignity was lost. It must when completed have been magnificent, and the garden as a whole must have been the finest in England. De Caus's plan has disappeared now, of course—even had it not it would be quite impossible to keep up such a garden under modern conditions —but it became so widely known throughout England that everyone who could afford to do so copied it. But for the most part what was copied was not the third division, but the close-knit rectangles. More and more and more rectangles, that was the Restoration fashion.

Naturally, many famous people have been here. The only two I can remember are Sir Philip Sidney and Shakespeare. Shakespeare acted here before James I, a fact I was told (for some reason) at my preparatory school and which I have never forgotten. Here Sir Philip Sidney wrote part of his *Arcadia*

for his " Dear Lady and sister, the Countess of Pembroke ".
And in this connexion there is romance indeed.  At the
beginning of the century there was found in the library here
between the leaves of a copy of the *Arcadia* a lock of Queen
Elizabeth's hair and this inscription :

> This locke of Queen Elizabeth's owne Hair was pre-
> sented to Sir Philip Sidney by her Majesty's own fair hands
> on which he made these verses and gave them to the Queen
> on his bended knee.

### ANNO DOMINI 1573

> Her inward worth all outward show transcends.
> Envy her merit with regret commends ;
> Like sparkling gems her virtues draw the light,
> And in her conduct she is alwaies bright.
> When she imparts her thoughts her words have force,
> And sense and wisdom flow in sweet discourse.

In the grounds of Wilton House, hard by a magnificent
stretch of water filled with fine fish—and that is as it should be,
for Wylye has among fishermen almost the fame of Itchen and
Test—stands The Daye House.  This was once the Dairy
of the big house, but has long been a private residence.  A
singularly attractive one it makes, too.  Though, hidden
behind high gates and closely bounded by tall dark trees, it
sometimes needs little imagination, especially on a really wet
day, to conjure up the sinister.  In summer, however, every
prospect is indeed fair.

Here lived and died Edith Olivier.  She had built on to
the original house at right angles a long wooden room, which
was part reception-room, part work-room, and here, reclining
on a divan she would hold court with her visitors.  Edith
Olivier was a most remarkable woman.  In an age devoid of
" characters " she was a " character ".  But also she was full
of character.  There was no pretence whatever about her.  I
knew her only towards the end of her life—the last ten years
or so—and every time I met her I was struck afresh with the

rapier-like quality of her mind, and the infectious merriment that was in her chuckle. She was small, tiny would be a better word : she had very piercing black eyes and a sharply hooked nose and a sharply pointed chin. There were occasions when she used too much paint and powder. There were occasions when she looked horribly witch-like. She could, I imagine, strike terror into the unwary, the timid, the gauche. But she was in fact kindness itself. She would always maintain that she was uneducated. It is true that her spelling had on occasions to be seen to be believed, and that her punctuation could be erratic in the extreme. But these things are common to the female sex as a whole and certainly not a sign of education lacking. She would always maintain that she had no knowledge of the English grammar. But if that was so, she yet managed to write beautiful limpid English prose. And she had more than a passing knowledge of the Classics, and could produce odd tags of Latin verse in the most disconcerting manner. When I was editing *The Field* she would sometimes come and see me in my office. She would sit in a chair much too big for her and smoke very cheap cigarettes out of a very long holder, and then get me to take her to lunch at one of the places " her friends would not approve of ". When I went to a meal as her guest, matters were very different. Then only the very best was good enough, both of food and cigarettes.

A writer of distinction, she never got the renown or the sales that she deserved. One novel, *Dwarf's Blood*, must rank very high indeed. It should not be allowed to be forgotten. But Edith Olivier was more than a novelist : she was also a public servant with an intense desire to serve the community in which she lived. You could not be in The Daye House for more than a moment or two without realizing that she had on more than one occasion held office as Mayor of Wilton. There are not many small country towns that can boast a Mayor. The few that there are are all very ancient, and by far the oldest of them is Wilton. It was, indeed, no small honour for Edith Olivier to be elected Mayor of Wilton.

In the old days, and up to I believe the Crimean War, it was an offence for the Mayor of Wilton to appear outside his door without his official red robe. If he did he was fined rather heavily by his own Corporation. Now the great robe is kept only for ceremonial occasions. I have seen the Wilton robe, indeed all the Wilton regalia. The robe is a very rich pure red, almost dazzling in its brilliance. And it hangs in great heavy folds which throw deep shadows. On Edith, for it was not designed for so small a person, the folds were very deep. But Edith lost no dignity so arrayed. On the contrary she seemed to gain in stature the more she was dwarfed, and her rather witch-like countenance took on the regal lines of a Phœnician princess. Even the immensely heavy silver-gilt chain of office seemed to hang lightly upon her. From this chain there hangs a jewel, upon which is emblazoned in blue enamel and gold the ancient seal of the Mayor. Nobody seems to be quite sure what this seal represents. At the Herald's Visitation of Wiltshire in 1623 it was described as "two Saxon kings *sejant* in Gothic niches, crowned with sceptres in their hands". But there are those who think that it depicts the Coronation of the Virgin. Whatever it is, it is a very fine jewel. Wilton also possesses some beautiful silver-gilt maces. One of these is of the time of Charles I and is a most delicate piece of work, another of the time of Charles II is huge and elaborate and must be one of the finest examples of the smith's art of that period to be seen anywhere in England. The Mayor's personal mace is of the reign of Queen Anne, of silver and small. There is a hidden cavity in its head, and Edith used to think that it was also used to carry disinfectant herbs in time of plague.

Edith Olivier with her profound sense of history was very conscious of the ancientness of Wilton, and well aware of all its ancient customs, many of which have fallen into disuse. One she revived. Before the old parish church fell into ruins, loaves of bread used to be given away to the poor people of Wilton on every New Year's Day. This custom Edith revived. She had a double reason for doing so. First because it was an ancient custom, and she disliked seeing old customs die out, and, secondly, because she was the first Lady Mayor, and the Saxon meaning of the word " lady " was " loaf-giver ". So she put on her red robe and took up her stand at the church door and distributed bread to the poor of the parish. I hope that the custom has not been allowed to lapse again now that she is gone.

She was a great woman. Great in its true sense. To-day so many of the would-be great are conscious of greatness. You may always tell them, for they do not suffer fools gladly. They are proud of this attitude : it gives them a sense of superiority they would find impossible to achieve otherwise. They forget that we are fools, all and each of us—if not in all things, then in more things than those in which we can claim wisdom. Edith Olivier was not of these. With more accomplishments than most, with infinitely more intelligence than most, she suffered all people except the consciously great or clever. To them she could be scathing indeed.

On the other side of Wilton lives another friend of mine. It would be worse than a crime to visit Wilton and not walk the odd quarter of a mile out to Ditchampton Farm to call on A. G. Street. Not the least of Edith Olivier's many benefactions to humanity was her discovery of Arthur Street. Arthur would have been discovered sooner or later anyhow, I know. He is not the sort of man who could possibly be overlooked. But the step from writing short articles in the local paper to writing a book for a leading London publisher is not an easy one to make, too often takes many years to make. It was shortened by Edith Olivier, who knew a good thing when she saw one, to the great benefit of the English nation as a whole. Our literature would be the poorer if it contained no *Farmer's Glory*.

So, hot and dishevelled, carrying my forty-pound ruck-sack, I walked unannounced into Ditchampton Farm. Deck-chairs on the lawn under the tall limes looked inviting, and a knock on the door brought the excited barking of a cocker spaniel and the bass roar of Arthur Street from some distant back room. Then a wash and seats on the lawn and a long cool drink under those limes and then another and another.

171

And conversation : I know no man in all England (and my acquaintances are many up and down the land) who can talk as Arthur Street can talk. He has an immense zest for life, a profound curiosity, a quirking stabbing brain, and a rich slow Wiltshire brogue that altogether belies the sharpness of the mind that controls the tongue. I am myself quite unable to hold Arthur in conversation. I am always two or three points—and sometimes two or three subjects—behind. If I try to talk too I am lost. While I am turning over and savouring some particularly shrewd remark, and trying desperately to think of something almost as brilliant to say, I have missed some other equally shrewd thrust. It needs the hover-fly quickness, the darting flight and sudden hover, the sideways glance, of a Reggie Arkell to cope with this huge, deceptively slow Wiltshire farmer. I no longer try. I sit and listen, trying desperately hard to remember something, so that I can try to work it off on somebody else as my own. Unfortunately I have not got that sort of mind. My memory for some things is not at all bad : I have the sort of memory that can docket page references in books, remember addresses and telephone numbers, the way about towns I have only been in once before. But I am quite unable to remember a good story a couple of hours after I have heard it or a good quip an hour later. Even so it is a joy to listen to a really good storyteller, and Arthur Street is one of the best. But sandwiched in between the stories and the quips there is a vast store of rural wisdom. Generations of stored, and painfully acquired, knowledge have come to the surface in this man and to it he has added the knowledge that quick observation and personal experience alone can bring. There are many who do not relish Arthur Street's views on modern agriculture, yet more who do not relish his views on modern political farmers. In modern England we have become afraid of criticism and our leaders to-day are born humourless. They have a " call " instead and it is a damned poor substitute. Arthur Street is nothing if not outspoken and no one on earth could accuse him of lacking a sense of humour. It is no wonder that he is not always regarded as " one of the boys ".

But, on this evening, while I was eating a good supper farmers from Yorkshire called to see him. And they did not do that because they disagreed with him. Moreover, this tenant-farmer has by his writing and his broadcasting done more than any other man to make the townsman aware of the countryman and his place in the general scheme of the national life, his work and his worries. There were countrymen writing before Arthur Street, of course, but none was listened to in his lifetime, not even Richard Jefferies. There have been many since *Farmer's Glory* was published, some good and some so bad that it is a marvel that any publisher even considered them, and quite a few have broadcast also. The country does get a hearing now in millions of urban homes. But we have, all of us, climbed on Arthur Street's shoulders. He is the pioneer, and we should not forget it.

I got my dinner, too—the best I had eaten since the walk started—and was then driven back into Salisbury to the Crown. I wanted a hot bath. It was getting late now, but there were still several stories to be told, and the lounge was empty and comfortable. I put my bath off to the morning.

The next morning was brilliantly fine and warm. I dallied over my breakfast, watching a honeymoon couple—only just married I was sure—trying to pretend that they had been married for years. In fact they did not know each other well at all, and could not have known each other for any length of time, because the girl could not remember whether the boy took sugar in his tea and the boy, ordering the meal, did not know whether the girl took coffee or tea with her breakfast. Moreover, neither was reading the paper. They were a nice pair, and the waitress served them with devoted and rather tearful attention. I was trying to make up my mind whether I should walk out and see Bert Walters and cadge another free meal, or whether I should walk on down to the coast. It was not an easy decision to make. Duty called me southwards : but I remembered with longing a meal at West Farm, I remembered a flock of Hampshire Downs, I remembered the lovely walk along the Harepath, the wind cool and the larks busy, I remembered one of the pleasantest days of my life.

That had been a couple of years before. I was doing a walk for the B.B.C. I'd spent the night sleeping out, and a cold night too, and I walked from Shaftesbury to Salisbury on one of the hottest days of a record-breaking summer. So hot, I remember, that I had stripped about mid-morning and bathed in the Ebble—greatly to the astonishment of a land-girl who happened to pass—and then I had climbed up to the Fovant Hut, and there Bert Walters met me with a car and beer. He did not know me from Adam, and I had never even heard of him. But he had worked out my route very accurately and timed it very accurately too, and there he was at just the right time with just the right stuff for a hot day and a man carrying a heavy pack. And all because I had used as the dust-cover for a book of mine a photograph of a flock of Hampshire Downs being led by the shepherd up on to the Downs, and that flock, though I did not know it, was Bert Walters' property and the place was the Fovant Hut.

Walters is a great man with the Hampshire Downs. His pedigree flock must, I imagine, have taken more prizes than any other in Britain. He is more than just an owner of pedigree sheep ; he is a flockmaster in the old tradition, one of the few—one of the very few—left here in the south of England. And I love sheep. I do not know anything about them, but of all farm animals I love sheep the best.

We disregard our sheep industry nowadays. Whitehall, which does our farming for us now, scarcely recognizes the sheep. And yet our sheep industry is really most important. In order of sheep population Britain ranks eighth among the nations of the world : only Australia, Russia, the United States, Argentina, New Zealand and India, in that order, rank ahead of us. (Actually, to-day, I suppose that we rank seventh, because India is now divided into Pakistan and India and neither has our population, though together they beat us.) Only Spain approaches us at all closely in sheep popula-tion among all the other sheep-producing nations of the world. That is surprising enough. But when you come to consider density of sheep population, then Britain ranks second in the world. New Zealand has the highest density of sheep per square mile, Britain comes next. I believe that it is true to say that New Zealand has round about twenty sheep for every human; Britain has one sheep for every two humans. We have in fact about 280 sheep to the square mile. The United States has about fourteen to the square mile. You would not think so, I know, just looking casually : but that is the fact.

It is a very old industry, too. It goes back at least to the Romans. The greatness and the prosperity of Britain was built up on sheep. It was the sheep that gave us the wool, and it was the wool that made us great, and it was the Romans who started the British wool industry. Throughout the Middle Ages we enjoyed great prosperity as a producer and exporter of wool to Europe. The sheep was not then regarded from any other aspect. Its flesh was not rated at all highly. It was a wool-producer only, though ewe's milk and cheese were quite important by-products. It was the Industrial Revolution that altered all that. The rapid increase in population caused an increased demand for meat, and the sheep became a meat-producer instead of a wool-producer. To-day, if we think of sheep at all (which is unlikely) we think of it in terms of mutton and lamb. It comes as a shock to most people to learn that one of the very few agricultural products we export is wool.

The Industrial Revolution brought about a great change in the distribution of our sheep. To-day, in the south of England, sheep are quite uncommon. In 1800 in Wiltshire it was estimated that there were more than half a million sheep on the Downs and about 120,000 on the Wiltshire pastures : in 1928 it was found that the population in Wiltshire worked out at about 250 sheep per 1,000 acres. The sheep population has, for the most part, moved north and west. The great sheep counties of the past—Hampshire, Wiltshire, Dorset, Norfolk—rank very low to-day. On the downlands now it is dairy cattle. Milk prices are more stable than mutton or wool prices. The dairy herd gives a steady monthly return.

Farmers love a steady monthly return just as dearly as anyone else.

But it was the repeal of the Corn Production Acts in 1921 that killed sheep farming in all those counties where light arable soils predominate. Farmers were forced to give up their flocks because of the low corn prices and the higher wage costs. Thousands of acres of arable land went down to pasture. The new pastures carried dairy cattle, and the sheep went north and west to the hill lands.

That was Whitehall policy, of course. It was shockingly short-sighted. If there had been any sort of constructive agricultural policy between 1921 and the outbreak of war in 1939 there would not have been the huge (and almost disastrous) decline in arable acreage. There would in 1939 have been many thousands of acres of light and medium soil in a condition of fertile arable cultivation through being periodically manured and trodden by folded sheep. It is true enough that the land sown to pasture had accumulated a store of fertility which was converted into grain (or rather it is true of that land which stock had used for supplementary feeding; it was not true of many ten-year-old and twenty-year-old pastures, for three crops proved conclusively enough that there was not much stored fertility there) but that makes no allowance for the cost of clearing. I do not know what that cost was. No figures have been published so far as I am aware, and I shall be astonished if figures are ever published. Whitehall will have forgotten them and gladly. But the cost must have been terrific. Countless thousands of acres had to be cleared, acres which the government, which successive governments, should never have allowed to become derelict. That cost should be set against the fertility. It would not make a pretty balance sheet.

We should not, of course, regard the sheep only as a meat-producer or only as a wool-producer. There used to be a saying about " the golden hoof ". We would do well to remember it again. Nor should we think, as we do—there is every sign that our present rulers have not really learnt the lesson of the years between the wars; their kindness for the farmer at the present moment is not dictated by a change of heart, but by lack of dollars—that the sheep is valuable now only on rough grazings. It is quite true that a large sheep population in Britain is best justified by the fact that so much of our total land area is between one and three thousand feet. Most of it lies in Wales, the north and north-west of England, and Scotland. It is not suitable for cultivation, for most of the ground is too rugged and the climate is too wet. It is not really suitable for cattle. It is, in fact, sheep ground. There should be no question at all as to the best way in which it can be utilized.

But it would be a grievous mistake to regard the sheep as useful only on rough grazings. We seem to have forgotten that sheep are far more efficient as converters of fibrous fodder to meat than are cattle. Sheep will eat the unconsumed growth of herbage on pastures, the vegetation in the stubbles, will crop the waste corners of the fields. Sheep will eat what cattle will not and where they will not. Sheep are less dependent on water supplies than cattle and much more fitted to cope with the vagaries of our climate. In fact, sheep should be kept on every farm. Not to compete with dairy cattle or intensive arable farming, but to prevent waste. I have no doubt whatever that sheep on the farm would result in better farming and increased production.

Equally I have no doubt that we shall not see any great increase in the number of sheep in Britain now. We may well see a decrease. The Forestry Commission has greedy eyes on the rough grazings. There is in many quarters in Whitehall a passionate desire to see Britain covered with huge conifer forests—but we go on importing pit-props !—but there is no passionate desire to see British farming prosper.

Feeling as I do about sheep, the desire to go out again to West Farm was very strong. But then I thought of the journey still to be made to the mouth of the river, the walk out and back and the day wasted (from the walking point of view), and suddenly I realized that this was a really fine day and that I ought to take advantage of it.

I went into the town and bought such supplies as it is

nowadays possible to buy without ration books and points
and all the other qualifications of a free Briton. It was not
much. And then I set out on the last leg, down Avon proper
to the sea.

## CHAPTER V

## TO THE SEA

THE actual junction of Ebble and Avon takes place at the village of Bodenham, about two miles south of Salisbury. You could easily miss it. From Salisbury to Bodenham the river is split up into any number of channels, and though on the map the main stream seems clear enough it is anything but clear which in fact is the main stream when you walk by the waterside. And, as a matter of fact, that itself is anything but easy to do. So that when I came to Bodenham I did not at once realize that this fresh stream was the Ebble (though I knew well enough that the Ebble joined here), it might so easily have been another side-runner rejoining the parent water.

The immediate surroundings of Salisbury on this side are dull. Only the spire, always there for the backward glance, relieves it. Once Britford, lying in a great curve of the river, must have been beautiful. Perhaps it still is, but all around now there is an indefinable air of impermanence, as though the Army had been here. I went, as in duty bound, to see the church. It is a Saxon foundation. Of that there can be no doubt. But I had read somewhere (probably in the *Highways and Byways* volume) that you could see Saxon work. I looked pretty hard and I could see none. I admit that I am no expert on Church architecture, and I may well have missed it, but if so it must be pretty small. Rather disappointed, I went to have a look at Longford Castle, the seat of the Earls of Radnor. This was not possible—but as I have been over the place before I was not so disappointed—and so I got to the junction of the Ebble and Avon rather quicker than I had thought would be the case. Starting much later than usual I had planned to get as far as Fordingbridge before nightfall, and to Christchurch the next day. But now I determined to make Ringwood by nightfall, and to dally a bit on the morrow.

Following closely the course of the river this would not be possible. But it is quite impossible to walk beside Avon between Salisbury and Christchurch. The river divides too often and you are always getting cut off by some channel or other. The most that I could hope to do was to cut down to it every now and again. Fortunately the road runs almost alongside the water for the whole of the twenty-eight or so miles. I was never out of sight of the river.

And from Bodenham the road to Matrimony Farm (a delightful name I always think for a farmhouse) runs so close to the water that it practically forms the bank. A footpath then takes you to Charlton All Saints, where the river broadens into a wide and fairly shallow pool. I do not know how many times I have been to this spot in my life—it must be some hundreds—but always I have seen cattle standing in the stream here. They were doing so on this occasion, and it was a hot day, so they had every reason to do so, but I cannot have come here only on hot days. I think that the shorthorns of Charlton All Saints use this pool as a sort of club. On the other side of the river (but which is the main stream? The weir seems to be situated on a runner, but there are so many channels hereabouts that it is impossible to say) in the woods on the hills is Trafalgar House, the eighteenth-century mansion, which a grateful nation gave to the first Earl Nelson, the brother of the Admiral, together with a number of other things, which, gratitude having grown cold (as gratitude always does), a later Government has taken away. Here are preserved, I understand, for I have never been in the house, Nelson's armchair, his couch, his telescope, his cane and one or two other relics. I wonder if anything is preserved here of the lady? In any case the nation's gratitude did not extend to her, though she played so big a part in the life of the Admiral, and therefore in his success.

I did not cross the river, but kept to the path that runs to New Court Farm, and so came to the road again at Castle

Mound, and here I did cross the river to go to Downton. I like the old Borough Cross and I have pleasant memories of the White Horse. I know many inns in England and Wales, and quite a few in Scotland, and more in Ireland. Not so much places that I have stayed a night in, but places where I have had a drink and some conversation. (There is a difference here that is not easy to put on paper. One of the nicest places I know for a drink and conversation, a place full of atmosphere and friendliness, is in the New Forest. It is also a hotel—at least for the summer months—and the beds are comfortable and the rooms are clean. But while I love it as an inn, I dislike it intensely as a hotel. As an inn a half-pint of bitter is sufficient passport for an evening if you feel so inclined : but go behind, and immediately the atmosphere has changed. Out of the bar you become a different person in the eyes of the landlord (or can it be his wife ?), you become a " visitor ", some strange rich being sent specially by a divine providence that looks after country inn-keepers, something to be milked.) I have not the least idea if this is also the case at the White Horse at Downton, for I have never stayed there. But I do know that there are few more pleasant inns to drop into. This morning there was a carter, crowing like mad because he had had to use his horses to pull a tractor out of difficulties, a commercial traveller playing darts with himself, and two hikers—a man and a girl—who eyed me with considerable distaste. They were properly dressed for the road, shorts and shoes, and a man who wore dirty grey flannels could not be a serious walker. I noticed that the girl had very hairy legs. She would have looked much nicer with them covered up, and she would have looked quite nice in a skirt. They were going to Salisbury, I found, and I told them that I was going to Christchurch. But beyond that conversation flagged. Then they saw my rucksack, and were intrigued by the sleeping bag, and the additional oilskin. They asked why I should carry two oilskins—a hint of amusement in the girl's eyes—but when I told them that it served me as a ground sheet, they became really interested. Sleeping out was something they had not thought about. (It always astonishes me

that so few hikers do consider sleeping out; that so many
people think that a tent is essential for a night outside a roof.)
They wanted to know if I did so regularly, and I said, yes I
did. I think that before I left that inn I had made two con-
verts. I felt sure about the man, not quite so sure about the
girl, who seemed to be much concerned about the incidence
of spiders on the ground at night.

When they left, I climbed the hill to the eaſt of the village
for my laſt look at Salisbury spire, silver above the woods,
and then came back into the village to take the road on the
eaſt of the river that leads to Woodgreen. On the whole this
road keeps closer to the river, during this ſtretch, than does
the main road, and in any case it is much quieter. In faƈt
between Downton and the Hampshire border I did not pass a
soul.

Immediately you are over the Hampshire border the
country becomes much more heavily wooded on the eaſt bank
of the river. Its whole charaƈter seems to change within the
space of a few yards. You are on heath now, the great
ſtretch of heathland that ſtretches from Southampton Water
almoſt to Dorcheſter, the heathland that bears the New
Foreſt, the heathland that gave Hardy his background.

> Yon heathy hill
> That rises sudden from the vale so green,
> The vale far ſtretching as the view can reach
> Under its long dark ridge, the river here
> That, like a serpent, through the grassy mead
> Winds on.

Southey's poem, "For the Banks of the Hampshire Avon",
is not regarded, I believe, as among his beſt. But he knew
his country well. Northward of here, the hills are light.
You look at the creſt of a ridge in Wiltshire and it is light-
seeming, even on a dark day. You look at the creſt of a
ridge here and it is dark, even on a bright day. The countryside has changed, and so have the men, and so have the farm
animals. You come off the chalk hills, out of the chalk
valleys, into a different world.

This is not, of course, the aƈtual New Foreſt. It is outside

STANPIT MARSH

HENGISTBURY HEAD

the official boundaries. But it is New Forest in character. Not the New Forest of the stockbrokers and the big cars and the nicely-schooled, nicely-groomed, docile ponies; not the New Forest of the golf-clubs and the bridge-clubs and the sherry-parties; not the New Forest of the money-conscious. But the New Forest. The New Forest that has small, dark, secretive men and quick brown-skinned women; the New Forest that has not altogether, even yet, lost the Celtic lilt to the speech; the New Forest of the commoner and the squatter and the Gypsy; the New Forest that can be very dark and very frightening in some moods. You are only one mile south of Downton—Downton, where the mother of all Parliaments was held—but the oaks and firs mark the county boundary most effectively. You look northward to downland; you look south and east and west to wild grey heaths and purple moors, and dark lonely conifer forests. There is a difference in the air, too—a hint of the sea about it, a more determined nip when it blows.

And so soon as you cross the Hampshire border you become aware of a greater wealth of wild life. I was at once aware of more bird song, and the songs of more kinds of birds as well. I was at once aware of the flies, many more flies or many more species. I was at once aware of the butterflies and the dragon-flies. And, hard by Hale House, a square grey house with a wonderful view across the many channels of Avon, I came across the droppings of roe deer, where they had crossed the road to drink from the river, and, a few yards further on, the droppings of fallow deer. There were curlew in the tufty grass by the river. This is wild country, wild indeed compared with Wiltshire, a mile or so back.

At Woodgreen I turned right to walk past the Mill and the Shallows to Breamore. "Bremmer" is the correct local pronunciation. There is a wide open green with a shallow brook running across it and a pool, where the cattle gather in the evening, and there is the blue ribbon of the main Salisbury road. Pretty enough, but Breamore has a church that no one should miss on any account. For this is a Saxon

N

church that *has* got Saxon remains still. Even without them it is worthy of attention, for it is a really beautiful little village church. The tower was originally supported by four Saxon arches, and one of these remains with its curious lettering and cable moulding, which the experts say dates from the eleventh century. The lettering reads, " Here the covenant becomes manifest to thee ". But it needs an expert to decipher that. Actually the inscription was once much longer than that, but now there are only the scraps of a few letters left. Naturally there is a good deal of later work in the building—one would not expect anything else—but in the main this is the original church. There are several Saxon windows and there is also a very battered stone rood, one of the very few specimens of ancient sculpture that modern experts are prepared to accept unreservedly as Saxon.

Away to the west of Breamore lies some very interesting country—Rockbourne, the Martins, South Damerham (the view from South Damerham is one that can hardly be surpassed in all Hampshire)—but I had to get on to Fordingbridge. I kept to the main road for the short two miles, and in that space was offered six lifts by holiday-makers in cars. I could have done with the lifts, for I do not really like walking main roads, and especially not one that leads to Bournemouth. The number of coaches astonished me, and also the number of people who wear paper hats when riding in coaches. Here on the west bank of the river, you are out of the New Forest altogether (though the soil is still very much Forest soil), but you look eastwards at the Forest proper. First at Godshill Inclosure, and then through a gap to the bare expanse of Ashley Walk, where, when I was a boy, the black grouse still came to the lek, and then at Sandy Balls. And as I walked, I regretted that I had stayed on the west of the river. The other side looked so attractive, and there would have been no danger of getting mown down by some vast motor-coach (there was imminent danger for the whole two miles from coaches tearing down to Bournemouth), but mainly because I was feeling home-sick. I know the downland and I love the chalk, but I am a New Forest man at heart. I know the feel of the poor thin light soil, I know the birds and the animals and what they are about, I know what the wind in the trees means, I am more in sympathy with the dark people than I am with the big flaxen-haired red-faced Saxons.

And I was thinking all that between dodging the motor-coaches, when I came into Fordingbridge. Fordingbridge is very very old. You would never think so to look at it. There is practically nothing old-world about it. Modern villas, and brickfields, and allotments ; Fordingbridge gives the impression that it is going to catch up with Bournemouth one day. I believe that they still make sails here, but the modern industry is angling. The Avon cannot compare, anywhere in its length, with the Test or the Itchen as a trout stream, but from here southwards it has the best salmon-fishing in Hampshire, and produces the heaviest salmon of any river on the south coast, and pretty well of any river in England. I have known more than one fish of 40 lb. and more taken from this river. But it is as a pike stream that it is still more famous. The pike do not run to the size of the fish of the Irish loughs, of course ; nothing near it. But there are a great many large pike in the water, and twenty-pounders are not regarded as particularly remarkable, though I believe that, in fact, a 32-lb. fish is the record rod-caught for the river. As a coarse-fishing water there is none more famous in all England. Pike, roach, dace, perch, chub all grow to a large size. Almost all the heavy chub are caught on the Avon ; the record dace for the British Isles comes from the Hampshire Avon, and many fish of about 1 lb. 6 oz. have been taken from its waters ; perch running round about 4 lb. are not so uncommon as one would think from looking at the records ; and the roach run surprisingly heavy as well. Moreover, recently there have been some big barbel taken in the lower reaches. The record British barbel comes from Christchurch, a fish of more than 16 lb., and the number of barbel of more than 14 lb. taken from one reach alone cannot be equalled anywhere else. The barbel were introduced into the Avon by an Irishman about the year 1900, but it is only within the last fifteen years or so that the effect of this enthusiast's initiative has been felt, and he did not unfortunately live to enjoy the fruits of his own imagination.

When I was a boy, fishing on the Avon was easy. You just turned up and fished. Even for salmon it was not so very difficult to get a day, and if you had to pay it was not expensive. But for coarse fish you could hop over from the heart of the Forest without ever warning anyone that you were coming, get down on the river and fish. If you liked you could hire a boat, and that was not beyond the pocket of a schoolboy on holiday. Times have changed. I do not know what the salmon-fishing costs, but since the spring fish run about 25 lb. apiece I am quite sure that it is not cheap, and I suspect that it is now pretty hard to get a day anyhow. Nor is the coarse-fishing quite so free and easy as it used to be. The boatmen have realized that London newspaper proprietors (there was one who was notorious for miles down the river) are not so clever as they like to make out ; that you can milk a London newspaper proprietor who wants to fish a sight easier than you can get a sixpence out of a New Forest man. So boats, if your pocket was shallow, got harder and harder to obtain. But, of course, you could fish, if you knew how !

The other nice thing about the Avon is that you can lie and watch the pike on a warm day, great green monsters lying so close below that it seems you could touch them. But I remember a honeymoon couple who went for a row, and the girl lay in the boat, trailing her hand in the water. There was a swirl, the surface never broken, and a cry, and she was minus two fingers—just like that. One of those fingers had her engagement ring and her wedding ring as decoration. About three years later a pike of 26 lb. was taken on a plug, and when opened up there were the two rings. And they got her address out of the Visitors' Book and sent them back to her. So, though they look so close and so inviting, I do not try to touch them. I looked a bit this time. But the water was dark and I could see nothing, could only guess what might be going on in the depths. It is not always so. Once when I was a boy, lying in a boat, looking at the bottom

(I have always preferred looking at the bottom to fishing; my fishing is less conventional as a rule), I saw a big pike swimming slowly towards me and held cross-wise in his mouth was a smaller pike, but one big enough to make swimming difficult. The big fish was moving slowly. I had plenty of time to see what was happening. Childhood memories put the smaller fish at 5 lb. They put the big fish in the *enormous* class—but maybe they are wrong.

Below Fordingbridge the valley widens, and you pass into a quiet agricultural country. The country on both sides of the river is low hereabouts, but you get the impression that the widening of the valley is all to the westwards. The ground seems to rise to the east. It does do so, too, except for the gap at Mockbeggar leading through to Ibsley Common and the Dockens Water, but the rise is only a few feet really—the highest point between Fordingbridge and Ringwood on the east bank of the river is only some 200 feet above sea-level. That height is sufficient in comparison with the lack of height on the other bank to mislead entirely. And the impression is coloured yet more by the nature of the country. To the east it seems much wilder, and is in fact much wilder, than to the west.

Just south of Fordingbridge the Ditchend Brook comes into the Avon from the bare country of Ashley Walk. A gentle little stream the Ditchend, red-brown and placid, and filled with nice dace, it would hardly seem to add to the waters of what has now become a full-sized river. Yet with only the Allen River coming in at Fordingbridge itself, the Avon has grown hugely in the half-mile or so from the town. A mile and a half further south and the Latchmore joins the main stream, running down from Islands Thorns and the high ground by Eyeworth. A bigger water than the Ditchend—I have seen it looking quite angry at times—it, too, like all the Forest streams is red-brown and it holds some quite nice small trout. Again the Avon seems to gain surprisingly quite a fair amount of water, and the story is repeated once again with Dockens Water, the largest of the three, that comes down from Fritham. And then just before Ringwood itself the

Linford Brook runs in. Between Fordingbridge and Ellingham the Avon gathers to itself quite a deal of water in a quiet
way, and between Ellingham and Ringwood the Linford adds
more than one would imagine, so that by the time Ringwood
is reached the Avon has grown out of all knowledge, and
changed its character completely too. These little Forest
rivers are, indeed, misleading. You come across them almost
by accident, without warning. They are shallow and narrow,
for the most part, red-brown in colour and placid in tempera-
ment. There is nothing to suggest that they are more than
grown-up ditches. But follow them to their mouths—the
Lymington River, that you can jump so comfortably at
Brockenhurst, is big enough to carry the packet boats four
miles further south, and bigger boats than that too, if necessary. The Beaulieu River that you can jump so comfortably
at Dibden, suddenly becomes a big stream a mile or so further
down, and is a biggish river before another mile has passed.
The fact is that these little Forest streams carry a great deal
of water. And then, of course, there are endless little rills—
nameless all of them, and most of them too small even for
mention on the Ordnance Survey—that wind through rushy
bottoms to join the Avon, and each one contributes more
water than a casual glance would indicate. With every mile
now, with every half-mile, the Avon seems to become deeper,
to flow more purposefully. It has become much more silent
too, and that adds yet more dignity. But it still has many
side-runners. I have heard this stretch of the river from
Fordingbridge to the sea compared with the Warwickshire
Avon, and I have heard it compared to the Thames. I think
there is in the character of the water a likeness to the Thames,
and in the shape of the stream there is, perhaps, a little of the
Warwickshire stream, but the Avon has a character all its own.
It is a chalk stream proper in the number of side-runners it
supports, but it is a coarse-fish river in the true tradition in
the depth of its waters and the steady purpose of its stream.
There is, in fact, no other river in all Britain like it. I think
myself that the nearest approach is the Arun in Sussex, above
Arundel; in the quality of its water, that is, and the nature

of the stream. But the countryside bordering the two is quite different, and the Arun, though much swifter—it is an astonishingly swift stream—is but a child compared to the Avon.

Unfortunately, there is no real choice of routes from Fordingbridge to Ringwood. If you want to keep anywhere near the river you have got to walk the main road. The distance is just about seven miles, and it is easy walking, or would be but for the traffic. But I hate main roads. I cannot begin to say how much I hate them. I do not remember who described tar as " the black vomit of Satan ", but he was right. I can remember walking roads when they were pleasant ; pleasant to walk upon and pleasant to look at. They had colour then—white or brown or yellow or grey— and they had life. They were part of the landscape, and at the same time they enhanced the landscape. The white roads made the grass look greener, the grey roads threw up the purple of the moors, the yellow or the brown enticed you into the woods and made the woods the more mysterious. Enticed is the word. The old roads beckoned ever onward. They crept softly away. They were companionable. And, always, always, they beckoned, they drew you on.

I started walking, quite considerable distances too, when I was about eight or nine years old. My father was a great walker and believed in setting me on the right road as soon as possible. I remember that often we would walk the high road in preference to the path or the track. I remember that the hedges were filled with scent. I remember the little puffs of dust you kicked up as you walked, friendly dust. I remember stopping once at a lonely cottage in Shropshire, and being welcomed and given a flock-bed for the night. You used to be able to do that sort of thing all over England, if so be you did not want to sleep out. And the humblest inn then catered for " travellers " and would find you a bed and a meal, and give you a welcome. Most of the old inns have gone. They call themselves hotels now, and charge accordingly or do not let rooms for the night. And the cottages have learned from the inns. The cottage people are getting an urban mentality. It is all due to the roads being tarred. The modern hiker has no conception of what he has missed.

Who to-day would walk a high road in preference to a path or a track? It is not merely a question of traffic and the discomfort that that causes. It is the road itself. The modern main road has neither life nor colour. Seen from above it looks blue, a dull blue ribbon stretched across the countryside. But when you are on them they are black—black and dead and hard. When it rains they are shiny, and when the sun shines they are ebony. And all the time they are callous and apart. Nothing can live on the modern main road, not even a worm. And little, it seems to me, can live by the side of them. I remember when the hedges were filled with scent : to-day you have got to go up to the hedge and ram your nose into them to get any scent at all. And if it rains all insect-life is poisoned. The modern main road is naught but a channel of death. Death to the unwary human who ventures on them, death to the insect-life, death even to the fish in the streams, for the tar gets carried away. Hard and unsympathetic is the modern main road. You could walk the old roads and they were kind to your feet as they were kind to the feet of the beasts. Tar draws the feet—burning, blasting when the sun is on ; relentless and cold when it is not.

But if you want to go from Fordingbridge to Ringwood and keep close to the river you have got to put up with all this. And so I did. Through Ibsley, where the geese come down in winter if the weather is hard enough (they used to come down every year), to Ellingham, where Lady Alicia Lisle lies buried under the grey altar tomb by the south door. She was an old woman when she died. She died because she observed the ancient laws of hospitality—to give shelter to the traveller and to ask no questions. She hid two men from Monmouth's rebellion. Her husband had been the regicide Lisle, but she had aided many a distressed cavalier during the Civil War. Knowingly or unknowingly (and I think the latter) she hid these two men, was given away, and so faced Judge Jeffreys at the Bloody Assize at Winchester. The scene in Winchester Great Hall has been described often enough : the astonishment as the foul-mouthed judge raved at the old lady, the muttering of the Hampshire gentlemen, and the movement of one to protect her (for which he also paid with his life), the calm dignity of the old woman. Alicia Lisle was sentenced to be drawn on a hurdle to the place of execution and there burned alive. But Hampshire refused point-blank to carry out such a sentence, and Jeffreys dared not enforce it. He had had one rather unpleasant experience coming through the New Forest and he had something of respect for the determination of the ordinary Hampshire folk as a result, even though he could bully and browbeat the Hampshire squires. Alicia Lisle was reprieved as the result of the intervention of the Bishop and clergy of Winchester, and the presence of a large, silent but obviously threatening crowd of Hampshire countrymen and many New Forest men outside the judge's lodgings. But the King, in this case, would have none of it. Remembering his father's death, that is not surprising. Alicia Lisle had to die. But another sentence was substituted, for the King was told in no uncertain terms that the original one would bring all Hampshire to arms. On September 2nd, 1685, Alicia Lisle, aged and ill, stepped quietly from an upper window of the Eclipse Inn in the Winchester Market Square, hard by the cathedral, on to the block and was beheaded. Her body, carried back to Ellingham, was accompanied by hundreds of men all the way : a triumphal procession rather than a funeral cortège. Ellingham's church bears the date 1720 on the porch, which was the year when much restoration was completed, but Alicia Lisle's tomb was not touched.

A couple of miles to the south, the wandering streams of Avon unite to form a lake—a shallow, soggy depression—and here, too, the roads from Poole and Christchurch meet the railway that has come over the moor from Brockenhurst. Here, naturally, is Ringwood.

Ringwood lies some two miles outside the Forest boundary as it is drawn to-day. But the New Forest used to run up to the Avon, and Ringwood has never lost the strong Forest connection.  Fordingbridge, which is on the west bank of the river, has never been a Forest town, and has none of the Forest atmosphere.  But Ringwood, which is on the east bank, was a Forest town and still has some of the true Forest atmosphere about it.  Some, but not much ; the main roads have brought much with them, and most of it from outside the Forest.  Ringwood and Lymington used to be the two towns of the Forest—Brockenhurst and Lyndhurst were never towns and are not to-day, and now they are no longer villages either —and now they are both just outside the Forest boundary.  Ringwood is losing its Forest atmosphere, though it has not lost its Forest connection.  But Lymington, which was the ancient capital of the Forest, has never lost the atmosphere and, though Lyndhurst is now regarded as the official capital, has kept, despite all official rulings, the connection unimpaired.  So far as the Forester is concerned Lymington is still the capital.  It is to Lymington that the New Forest people go for the Saturday night spree.  But the people who come to Ringwood now are mainly tourists.

It is a very pleasant little place.  There is no suggestion of great age, but the houses are in character—there is an occasional old window, weathered tiles, old gables, some thatch—and the streets are narrow and the old market square is irregular in shape.  And above it all, the battlemented tower of the church gives at first sight a suggestion that there is a castle here.  In fact, the church is not more than one hundred years old.  There was a thirteenth-century church here, but it got into such bad repair that it had to be pulled down completely.  The rebuilt church, however, has fitted into the general scheme of the town remarkably well.

Ringwood market used to be a great occasion, and its fair (which dates from the fourteenth century) was a red-letter day of my boyhood.  The market has, of course, gone the way of all markets now.  And I have not been to the fair for more than twenty years.  In fact, the only thing that I could find of the old Ringwood that I knew was the beer—and that had certainly lost a little !  But the famous brewery is still there, and one day no doubt beer will return to beer.

I walked out of Ringwood towards the Forest and climbed the hill to Picket Post. Though this is not at all high as heights go—a mere 314 feet above sea-level—you get a real sensation of height. The moor is open and windswept, and you can see a long way. It can be very cold up here at times, and always there is the faint smell of the sea borne on the wind. A good place to sleep, if you can find a little shelter, and I knew just where to get that, for I have slept here often, and know the lie of the land very well indeed.

The next morning, while I was having my breakfast and preparing another cup of coffee, I became conscious of ants. Or rather I became conscious of a great activity among the ants. I am interested in ants, and normally notice those that are about—the species and so forth. I had, of course, noticed the ants around my sleeping place. And while I was getting my breakfast I had seen one or two ants of different species running about. But this was quite different. This was movement on a big scale. I do not know how long it had been going on when first I noticed it, but I do not think it could have been long, not more than a few moments. I feel fairly sure that I should not have missed for more than a few moments any largish movement. Be that as it may, when I did notice it, ants were all over the place. There seemed to be thousands of them.

Now, the New Forest is a very good place for ants. There are thirty-six species in Britain, and you can find most of them in the Forest. Some are in enormous numbers. *Ancanthomyops flavus*, the yellow ant or meadow ant, for example, occurs in millions. This is the ant that makes earth mounds, the ends of which always point east and west. There is one spot on Balmer Lawn where the mounds occur in profusion : over one hundred of them in a very confined area the last time I counted. There are other places in the Forest where you may notice the same thing. I became aware of ants at a very early age, and I have never ceased to be interested in them, and will always watch them if I get a chance to do so. They are in any case fascinating creatures, so fascinating that their study can become an obsession.

It has always been so. Man has always been fascinated and depressed and even alarmed by ants. Fascinated enough to draw analogies between the ant state and the human state (one of the most recent investigators has even been discussing seriously the question of communism or fascism among ants !) ; depressed because of their total submission to the will of the whole : alarmed by their astonishing efficiency. And, indeed, if you look at an ant, you cannot help but see that it is a formidable creature. There is, perhaps, little beauty about it—it depends what you mean by beauty— but there can be no doubt whatever that it is perfectly adapted functionally. It has two stomachs—the one personal, the other social ; it has a sting and a poison store ; it has two long antennæ, which combine the functions of nose and eyes, of tongue and compass ; it carries everything that it needs with it—brush and comb, sword and axe, shears and grinders ; and it is so adaptable that it can, as necessity dictates, use itself as a store, as a beast of burden, or as a door. And what a company of ants acting in consort can do almost defies cataloguing.

Physically, too, they are astonishing. Their strength in proportion to their size is immense (it has been worked out that the strength of the little garden ant is comparable to that of a man who could lift a two-ton lorry over a five-foot fence) : their speed is comparable to that of a man who could run at twenty-five miles an hour. Not only this : they are able to live without food for at least three months, and without air for a week. And if the head is severed from the body, the head will continue to fight, although there is no future in it. In fact, ants have been so successful that there are now over 3,500 species, none of which can interbreed. Their history is of immense length, going back millions of years before man appeared on earth. This means that their diversity is extreme. Especially is this so in size : some ants are more than a thousand times larger than others living in the same nest. Their adaptability is such that they can live anywhere in any climate. They are to be found all over the world from the Arctic to the Antarctic and at all heights. They are equally at home in lands of perpetual snow or in eternal deserts; in ships and houses as in jungles or lonely islands. Everywhere, in fact, except Iceland. Why that should be so, no one can tell, but the fact remains that they have not yet been recorded from that island. And their colonizing zeal is comparable to that of the British at their most energetic—more so, in fact. One example will be sufficient. *Iridomyrmex*, a tiny ant with a remarkably soft body, set out from Argentina fifty years ago on what can only be called a drive to conquer the world. It crossed the Atlantic and it has now reached Asia. It is established in the New Forest as well as in one or two other parts of England, and it seems to have come here from Guernsey. Yes, they are remarkable creatures. And not the least remarkable thing about them, with all their diversity, is that some exist to-day (and in large numbers) that are exactly the same as the ants found fossilized in the Baltic Amber of millions of years ago. No evolution there; no progress. But there is no need to evolve once perfection has been attained. We are a little too apt to forget that.

The ants I was watching on this morning were all *Formica sanguinea*, the large blood-red ant, and our only true slave-maker. There seemed to be thousands of them, and they were all going the same way. It took me a second or two to realize that. And then I went to see where they were going. But within a few yards, the column split—many going off half-left, while the remainder kept straight on. And a few yards further on yet the columns were halted and were massing up as more and more ants kept arriving. It was now quite clear what was happening. This was a mass raid on a nest of *Formica fusca*, the negro ant. I could see the *fusca* nest, and frantic activity on it. And then the *sanguinea* armies moved in to attack, one column from the front and one column from the rear—as well ordered and directed as if they had a commanding general placed in some strategic place.

The *fusca* workers put up some defence—a stout one, I imagine, for in my eagerness to see what was going on I put my head right down and got a few good shots of formic acid. But there was, I think, much panic. I watched some *fusca* workers, carrying pupæ, running up the grass stems and clinging there to be out of the way of the raiders. I saw other *fusca* workers killed by raiders. But the idea of the raiders was certainly not to kill—they did not go out of their way to chase any *fusca* workers making off, and only killed those that were actually in their way—but to capture pupæ and larvæ. They wished to gain entrance to the nest, and this they accomplished almost at once. In a very short time there were *sanguinea* workers returning with pupæ (it was almost always pupæ that were carried away; I noticed very few larvæ being removed) to their own nest, which was situated round the stump of a gorse bush close by my sleeping place. The distance between the *fusca* nest and the *sanguinea* nest was 116 paces (I paced it twice) and the *fusca* nest was slightly downhill from the *sanguinea* nest. That is a long way for an ant to carry a burden, but they covered the distance remarkably quickly—I did not time one journey however, for I had not got the sort of watch that would have done that accurately, and also there was so much to see at once that I did not want to miss any of it. The *fusca* nest, it seemed to me, was thoroughly ravaged. Very few pupæ could have escaped— a few up the grass stems, perhaps, and perhaps one or two workers succeeded in escaping with their charges to a safe distance, but I must say that I did not see any signs of this, and I did see one escaping *fusca* worker pursued and overtaken and killed. At the *sanguinea* nest there was great activity and excitement. But it all seemed to be very well ordered, the booty being taken below at once and the carrier either returning to the raided nest or disappearing below altogether.

This is the first time that I have watched a raid by *sanguinea*. I believe that such raids have been watched very infrequently in this country; only some half a dozen times in all. But they must occur comparatively frequently, since we know that *sanguinea* cannot get along without slaves. The time was 6 a.m., and I am wondering if it is the usual practice of this ant to make its raids before man is normally out and about. If it is that would account for the infrequent observations of what must be a fairly frequent occurrence.

Thoroughly cheered up by this, I packed up and set off
for Moortown and the main road to Christchurch. I was a
good hour later than I had meant to be, but even so I should
be in Christchurch well before lunch. But my excitements
for the morning were not over yet. Coming down off the
top by Foulford I disturbed a party of red deer, four hinds
about three years old. I was quite close to them when they
got up and I had a fine view of them as they made up the hill
and back to the Forest. I turned to watch them, and as I did
so a big dog fox crossed the path within a couple of yards of
me—I could smell him—and paused to look at me before
going on into the undergrowth. He was a really fine specimen, but grey rather than red, which meant that he was not
a Forest fox. Some years back a few hill foxes were introduced to the Hampshire downlands, and the dogs are great
travellers. It is curious, too, that the colour should remain
true all this while. I have noticed this in other parts of the
country and it is true also of some foxes introduced from
abroad. The zoologists will not have it that it has any
significance, but I must say that I believe that it has.

There are two roads from Ringwood to Christchurch—
the true main road on the east bank and a subsidiary on the
west bank. I was on the east bank, and it was a toss-up which
road kept closer to the river. They take it in turns, but on
the whole the map seemed to indicate that the east bank main
road had the better of it. So down the main road I went.
And early enough to miss the worst of the traffic. It is an
easy road, running through a low green valley. The Avon
corkscrews all over the place, sometimes running in at least
a dozen channels, and every now and then spreading out into
small shallow little lakes or larger rush-hidden swamps. It is
a great place for birds just here, and I have spent many hours
in winter watching them. In hard weather particularly you
get all sorts of waders up from the shore, as far as Bisterne
Park, but more usually not above Avon Tyrrell. There are
lots of little lanes running off to the east to the commons and
woods of the Forest area, and just before Sopley a road runs
west over the river to Hurn. Hurn is no longer a hamlet

scarcely known to the people of nearby Bournemouth. Its name is now known all over the world, for it is now a great airport. Surprisingly enough it does not seem to have made very much difference to the immediate neighbourhood, for you cannot go anywhere in Britain now without being aware of aeroplanes above you. Bird-watching in the valley you are far removed from the famous airport at your back ; you would not know that it is there.

Sopley is a pleasant little village—beautiful in the winter when the tourist traffic is at a standstill—and the church should be visited for just one historical association. Moreover, from the knoll on which the church stands there is a very good view of the Avon valley trees, fringed along the course of the river itself, all the way down to the estuary. In the church lies the body of Lord Keane. And that is now a name that means nothing to Englishmen. But Keane was the man who led the march to Kabul in 1839. England is dotted with the graves of gallant men who have been sent on ridiculous missions by the politicians in Whitehall, planning to deal with affairs that they know nothing about, but there can be no more blood-stained episode in all our history than this of Kabul, no more startling evidence of the effect of meddling in affairs of which you know nothing, of ignoring the advice of the man on the spot. Keane did what he was told to do. He went to Kabul. But he had to leave some of his men behind to aid the British Envoy there, and the rest of his force was cut to pieces in the Khyber. Here he lies in a quiet little Hampshire village, an eternal memorial to the ignorance of the politician. How much of our history is engraved in village churches !

At one time there used to be a light railway from Christchurch to Ringwood, and I crossed the river by the Hurn Bridge and got on to the track where it used to run, and so walked down to Christchurch, passing through the low-lying marshes below the bluff of St. Catherine's Hill. I know no better approach to Christchurch than this. The marshes are many-coloured—green and yellow and purple—Dorset lies away to the west and to the east the rolling hills and

VIEW FROM HENGISTBURY HEAD

heaths of the Forest, while southward the Priory rises grey from the mist of the estuary.

At Christchurch the Stour comes into the estuary from the Dorset uplands, forming a great stretch of water that once was a famous harbour. A good deal of our history started here. These south-coast rivers formed the gateway into England, and the Avon was not the least important of them. Indeed, in pre-Roman times, there can be little doubt, this was an important port from which goods were exported to the Continent. There seems to be little doubt that the Hallstatt culture of the Iron Age had much to do round here, and perhaps it even came into the country by this route. Their deeply-incised and fine hæmatite-coated wares have been found in some profusion on Hengistbury Head. And the fort on the Head was not put there for no purpose at all. It is magnificently situated for defence, the narrow neck cut by the ditches, and behind the expanse of Christchurch Harbour, making it almost impregnable. Later invaders also came this way. Hengist, on his second invasion, landed here—hence Hengistbury Head—and no doubt it remained a port usable by the small ships of those days for many years. Now, it is no longer a port, and the word "harbour" is but a courtesy title. The time when the south-coast rivers were the channels of commerce has long passed. Once goods were carried far inland and the produce of the countryside was brought to the ports by their means. Changed conditions of transport have altered the use that is made of rivers to-day. But the main factors in the decay of these southern rivers have been the wind and the weather and the silt. In many cases these have stopped their outlet to the sea altogether, in many others have made them unnavigable. Winchelsea and Pevensey in Sussex are good examples of the outlet being blocked altogether. In Hampshire, for the most part, the rivers have now become the playground of the fisherman : they have been lost to the merchant. But at Christchurch the harbour is now shut off from the sea by a sandbank that has formed through the centuries. The combined waters of Stour and Avon now find their way to the sea at Mudeford through a narrow channel,

known as the Run. The sandbank makes a great lagoon, a
huge sea-water lake, and that is much enjoyed by sailing
enthusiasts. It is interesting to note, too, the difference in
the type of boat used on the Stour and the Avon. The Stour
is a sluggish stream, and the pleasure boats are rowing boats
or punts, but on the Avon the canoe is the craft. From time
to time proposals have been made for opening up Christchurch
Harbour again. John Taylor, after making a journey by boat
from London to Salisbury in 1623, wrote in his *New Discovery
by Sea* of the trade that could be brought into Salisbury by
water if Christchurch Harbour was open. As a result in 1644
an Act was passed for making the river navigable. But
nothing was done. In 1674 Andrew Yarranton, in his
*England's Improvement*, said that he had been taken down the
Avon by Lord Clarendon to see if a safe harbour could be
made at Christchurch. He recommended the construction of
a great harbour, and work was actually started, for a pier and
a wharf were built shortly afterwards. But again nothing
came of it. Not long afterwards we find Defoe writing : " As
for Christchurch, tho' it stands at the mouth of the Avon,
which, as I have said, comes down from Salisbury, and brings
with it all the waters of the north part of Dorsetshire ; yet
it is a very inconsiderable poor place, scarcely worth seeing."
And now it is much too late to do anything. The silting is
going on all the time, and one day the lagoon will be a lagoon in
the full sense, and the waters will seep out through the sands.

Between Christchurch and Mudeford lies Stanpit Marsh,
one of the famous places on the south coast for birds and
particularly for the waders. Almost every rare wader has
been seen here at some time or another, and a visit to Stanpit
is always an excitement for you never know what you may
see. The marsh belongs to the town, and though there are
shooting rights over it, the town is conscious of the value
of the marsh and has recently saved it from exploitation as a
pleasure ground. There are after all more than sufficient
pleasure grounds but a short bus-ride away in Bournemouth,
a town that exists solely to provide pleasure for visitors.

I walked down to the Priory. I have a great fondness for

Christchurch Priory, so white and clean and fresh, and particularly for its situation. I would never go to Christchurch without visiting the Priory. And there is always the miracle to think about, and the way that it made Flambard, William the Red's unscrupulous justiciar, feel holy all of a sudden. Though, in fact, I am not sure that it made him feel anything of the sort : I think he realized that there was money in miracles. I do not in the least mind, for it gave us a fine church. Really, you want to stand on Hengistbury Head to get the proper view of the Priory, then you do realize to the full why it is called the Priory in the Marsh. Flambard was a rogue beyond question, but he was a genius at this business of church-building. You have only to think of Durham to realize how great a genius. And certainly he sited this Priory Church ideally.

As a church it is difficult to describe. It is not a whole in any sense, except when seen from a distance. It might best be described as a catalogue of the English styles of architecture, a collection of samples. But as a collection it includes only good work. Particularly fine is the Norman turret at the east end of the north transept. The great north porch must be one of the finest examples of Early English work to be seen anywhere in the country ; the windows in the south aisle are good Decorated ; the rood-screen, a glorious example of the stone-mason's art, is beautiful Perpendicular. And so you could go on. Christchurch Priory to be appreciated as it should be must be seen many times, each visit being devoted to the study of one portion. And each visit should also include a distant view of the whole.

As I came out again, a voice hailed me.

" Say ! We didn't think you'd remember."

I had not, as a matter of fact. But I went to a good Public School, and if they taught me nothing else—and they did not —they did at least teach me how to lie like a gentleman. I greeted Lotis and Ella, manicurist and lift-girl from Brooklyn. " Of course, I did," I said. " How could I forget ? "

I was hauled off to a café, where they had discovered that you could get good ices (and they were good too), and regaled me with an account of their adventures. " And have you bought sleeping bags ? " I asked. " And are you sleeping out ? "

" Ooh, yes," they chorused. " We bought bags in Salisbury. And we have slept out. We slept on Hengistbury Head last night."

" Good Lord. I am surprised." And this made them indignant.

" Why ? Why ? Say, if you can sleep out at your age, we can."

Abashed, I offered to show them the Priory. To my relief they had seen it. But what was I going to do ? I was going to the very end of the river. I was going to walk down to Mudeford and then out on to the spit, and then I was going to get someone to row me out a little way, so that I could say that I had really been to where the Avon entered the sea, and then I was going to be put down on Hengistbury Head, and then I was going to walk back to the ferry and get a bus into Bournemouth, and have a good meal and a bath. And, I said, firmly, I am going alone for this walk. This is work, not play. " O.K.," they said, they weren't the sort of girls that forced themselves on men who did not want them. But we arranged to meet in Bournemouth Square that evening and have dinner together.

I set off for Mudeford. Marsh joins meadow here. Reeds cover shingle. It is very flat and very lonely in the winter and it can be very cold. To the east the low yellow cliffs show up, and before you is the steep mound of Hengistbury. Away over the bay you can see the jagged outline of the Needles. It is a lovely walk. I know only one better on the Hampshire coast and that one I am keeping to myself.

Mudeford set out to be a popular seaside resort. It has never achieved that. Barton and Milford seized the fashion. So Mudeford has remained a rather pleasant little place, bypassed for the most part by the crowds. The speculative builder has not been absent, but it is not so bad as many places I could mention on the coastline of my county.

I walked out on to the spit. The swans were there as

usual. There are always swans here—sometimes in winter quite a large herd of them—and on this afternoon there was also a great black-backed gull, though what on earth it was doing there at this time of year I do not know. Men were sailing, and there was a young man practising in a canoe, going along at a most fantastic pace. He was, I was told, practising for a solo channel crossing. When I asked a man to row me a little way out to sea so that I could see where the river came in to the sea, he thought I was mad. Rucksack-laden, I suppose that it must have seemed a strange request. But he did it. And when I had seen all that I wanted and asked him to put me down on the sand below the cliffs of Hengistbury, he agreed without a murmur. Rowing me there, he said suddenly : " You know, if you'd been here back in March you'd have seen a whole flock of spotted redshank." " How do you know that I'm interested in birds ? " " Listen to the wireless," he said. " 'Sides, I've seen you on Stanpit, I remember now." The boat grounded on Hengistbury but we sat in it for a long time, smoking and talking birds. And when I got out to climb up the old fort, and turned to pay him, he would have none of it. " Stand me a drink next time you're round," he said, and pushed off.

Heart-warmed by so much friendliness, I made the stiff climb. It is stiff too. And on the top I looked again at Christchurch Priory rising so grandly from its marshes, and thought for a moment of the bathes I had had here when I was a boy, and of the tales of the smugglers that I had listened to from old Catchlove, a boatman who bore a grand old smuggler's name and looked, with his one leg, like John Silver himself.

Lotis and Ella were waiting in the Square at Bournemouth. They had dolled themselves up. They looked very smart indeed. American girls certainly know how to wear clothes. No doubt these dresses were really quite cheap ones—I would not know anyway—but both young women were looking very pretty and the clothes looked to me to be pretty good too. I looked down at my old grey flannels, and noticed for the first time that there was a great rent in the right knee. My boots were dirty, my coat old and patched, my shirt khaki and open-necked and dirty. My rucksack stained.

"Well, where'll we go?" they asked. "You know this place?"

"Oh yes," I said. "I know this place all right. There's nowhere I can go here with you two dressed up like that. Only the cafés in Bournemouth would put up with me to-night. And you're dressed for the bright lights."

"And we're damned well going to see them, too," they said. "Which is the best place for a meal and all that goes with it?"

Furthermore, they would not hear of meeting me afterwards. We would eat together or not at all, and they would not eat in a café. They had not hired a room in Christchurch to get themselves up in my honour to be pushed off with a "dime a time".

So I marched up to the Norfolk, my heart in my mouth. I had stayed there in the past, but under rather different circumstances so far as dress was concerned, and liked it. But knowing the British hotels' reactions to walkers dressed for walking, I was not too hopeful. I relied on the company of my two beautifuls getting me past. It was only just as I went through the door, past a very astonished-looking hall-porter, that I realized that they would probably not associate the two girls in those dresses with me in my torn trousers.

There was a waiter inside—by his tie, the head waiter. I went up to him, followed by the girls. "I want," I said firmly, "dinner for three." There was not a flicker on his face as he answered. "Yes, sir. Have you booked a table?" And when I told him that I had not, he said, "Then I am afraid that you will have to wait a little until one is vacant."

"That's all right," I said. "I want a bath, and these two want drinks."

The word "bath" did astonish him a little. But he recovered quickly. "I am sure that can be arranged, sir," he said, "and if you ring for the lounge waiter he will attend to your drinks."

I sat the two of them down in the lounge, ordered them their drinks and went over to the reception office. " I want a bath," I said. The girl behind the counter did look astonished—her mouth fairly dropped open for a moment—but she, too, recovered herself at once. " Are you stopping in the hotel ? " she asked, stalling for time. " Oh no," I said. " Just in for dinner, but I'm rather dirty and I would feel better if I had a bath." " Yes, sir." And she rang a bell and got a page, and had me shown to a bathroom.

It was a good bath. It was a good dinner. It was a grand evening altogether. And particularly good it was to find that there are still hotels in England, luxury hotels, that are staffed with people with manners and that extend hospitality to the traveller. There was nothing about me at all that could possibly have suggested a tip. It made not the slightest difference to the service I received. And I enjoyed myself the more for the knowledge that it did not.